# THE PLEASURE'S ALL MINE

*The Memoir of
a Professional Submissive*

JOAN KELLY

CARROLL & GRAF PUBLISHERS
NEW YORK

*For, and because of, Terry Wolverton and Women at Work.*

THE PLEASURE'S ALL MINE
*The Memoir of a Professional Submissive*

Carroll & Graf Publishers
An Imprint of Avalon Publishing Group Inc.
245 West 17th Street
11th Floor
New York, NY 10011

AVALON

Copyright © 2006 by Joan Kelly
First Carroll & Graf edition 2006

Library of Congress Cataloging-in-Publication Data is available.

ISBN-10: 0-7867-1648-7
ISBN-13: 978-0-78671-648-7

Printed in the United States of America

*Interior design by Pauline Neuwirth, Neuwirth & Associates, Inc.*

Distributed by Publishers Group West

# THE PLEASURE'S ALL MINE

# ONE

**"WE'LL START TODAY'S** demonstration with a few basic principles about mummification."

The little man spoke confidently to the audience from a small, mostly bare stage. I felt my face redden as I listened, even though I had no idea what mummification actually meant. *Thank God they turned the lights down first,* I thought, *bad enough to feel like the squarest person in here, without being caught blushing for no reason.*

I'd tried to talk myself out of coming to this anonymous-looking movie theater in the Valley all morning. I'd never been around a big group of kinky people like this before, nor had it ever been a particular life-goal of mine. But I had been trying to meet another suitable man ever since breaking up with my first sexually dominant partner several months earlier. I could not stand one more blind date from the Internet with one more "SexyMaster-forYou" who turned out to be someone else's straying, dorky husband. It seemed like the only logical choice was to get out of the house and mingle with other sadomasochists in their natural habitat—North Hollywood.

I'd done an online search for kink support groups and had found the Web site for Threshold, the group that was putting on this mummification certification class, or whatever the hell was going on here. Threshold, I'd learned, had been around for ten years or so, throwing regular parties that were the equivalent of singles mixers for bondage-and-discipline types, and their new-member orientation meetings were held on Sunday afternoons. This would give me plenty of time to scope out the scene and still get to bed early that night. I had to be up at the crack of dawn for my executive secretary job during the week.

I'd been a glorified receptionist for almost two years, and did not expect to meet a kinky soul mate at the conservative nonprofit agency where I worked. I didn't go to church or belong to a gym either, nor was I masochistic enough to sign up for swing dancing lessons at the local community college. In short, I rarely met anyone to date at all, let alone someone who shared my sexual interests. I worried that I might have lost my one chance when I broke things off with the only kinky boyfriend I'd ever had. Hoping I might be wrong about that, I'd made the drive out to the Threshold event and seated myself toward the back of the medium-sized movie theater.

From the tone of his voice, I thought the man with the microphone was smirking, but it was hard to see his expression clearly due to his handlebar mustache. "Although this kind of activity is somewhat labor-intensive, you can make it easier on yourself by having your slave do most of the prep work the night before," he continued. I listened with increasing confusion as he described a process of cutting up sheets and mixing cornstarch and water to make the necessary supplies for turning one's sexual slave into a mummy.

Labor-intensive? That didn't sound very exciting to me. Where was the deep-voiced, slightly imposing older man asking for shy but pent-up female volunteers from the audience for God knows what kind of twisted pleasures on the stage in front of us? Where was the

"The wisdom of St. Bernard has found an outstanding new voice in the meditations contained in this book. The author's wonderfully personal style transforms the reader from a mere listener to an active participant in a grace-filled dialogue. The experience of monastic life appears here in all of its beauty, simplicity, and truth."

—Fr. Maximos of Simonopetra (Mt. Athos)


"Long ago St. Francis espoused Lady Poverty and in our own time Bernard Bonowitz, OCSO, has taken to himself Lady Truth. The happy fruit of this union is a commentary that conveys St. Bernard's meaning in a way that brings us in touch with the original depth, incisiveness and humor of this great work. We are deeply indebted to Bernard Bonowitz for making this possible by his own honesty, humor and depth."

—Mother Maureen McCabe, OCSO
Mount Saint Mary's Abbey, Wrentham, Massachusetts
Author of *I Am the Way: Stages of Prayer in Saint Bernard*


"Dom Bernard offers an analysis so clear and compelling that this book will become a spiritual 'source book' for all who read it. There is a depth of personal experience and conviction in the book that is captivating. With sweeping references to literature, philosophy, and theology, Dom Bernard demonstrates a breadth and depth of appreciation for the spirituality of Bernard of Clairvaux that balances scholarship with spiritual direction."

—Fr. James McCloskey, CSSp
Duquesne University


"This book has much to recommend it, especially as a reliable interpretation of the Saint's teaching. In a particular way, it will help us to discover how the doctrine of the Abbot of Clairvaux is present and active in our own monastic life as we live it in the here and now. The examples taken from the author's personal experience give a special zest to the solid teaching the book contains, all of which contributes to the depth and relevance of its message and the attractiveness of its general style."

—Abbot Bernardo Olivera, OCSO
Abbey of Nuestra Señora de los Ángeles (Argentina)
Author of *The Sun at Midnight: Monastic Experience of the Christian Mystery*

bondage, the discipline, the sadomasochism, for Pete's sake—the "BDSM" mentioned on the Threshold Web site?

I looked around to see if I was the only puzzled member of the audience and noticed a man who bore a striking resemblance to "T," the dominant man I had recently stopped seeing. My throat tightened and I looked away—could it be . . . ? No. I stole another glance and saw that he was, in fact, a stranger. The hair was similar—a full head of it, brown, parted in the middle, and trimmed to above the ears—and the profile showed the same strong chin and straight nose. But the man in the theater was clearly taller than T, which was apparent even while he was seated. When I wore four-inch heels, T and I stood almost eye to eye. He had always *felt* bigger to me than he really had been.

I shook my head and forced my attention back to the boring presentation. The man with the microphone had set it down and was dipping small pieces of cloth into a bucket filled with white goo. Another fellow was lying still and quiet on what looked like a hospital gurney in the center of the stage, in pre-mummy nakedness.

"Who wants to give it a try?" The lecturer beckoned the audience to join him on the stage, either as an additional mummy or as a mummifier. About a dozen men and women got up to join him.

I sunk a little lower in my chair, trying to face the undeniable fact that I'd been uncomfortable here since I'd arrived. Most of my fellow audience members had trickled into the theater in couples consisting of one obviously dominant and one obviously submissive person. Many men and women had a length of slim chain between them, as one held the end of a leash that led to a collar the other was wearing. There seemed to be an almost equal amount of dominant men and dominant women among them, and an equal amount of gestures between them that made me cringe.

Before the demonstration started, a man a couple of rows in front of me had whined softly at the woman who still held onto his leash, even though they were seated.

"But I just got comfortable," he fake-pleaded, rolling his eyes in exaggerated disgruntlement. "Ouch!" he yelped, as the woman pinched his ample waist.

"You still too comfortable to get up and get me that water like I told you?"

The man scowled as he rose from his chair, and the woman giggled, as did the couple seated next to them. I had encountered a similar mentality on the online bulletin boards I'd visited in recent months, looking for clues from other women who identified themselves as being submissive, as well as the dominant men who flocked to them. It seemed to me that being submissive, to some people, indicated a willingness, if not an outright desire, to be treated like a bratty child. I didn't even like the way most people treated real-life bratty children. I certainly didn't want to fuck someone who thought foot-stamping and swift retaliation were suitable acts of foreplay.

If I was going to let somebody boss me around, especially in public, I'd want them to be doing things that relaxed and excited me, not put me on guard. Maybe a deep voice ordering me quietly to do things, tugging gently but insistently at the hem of my shirt or zipper of my jeans, warm hands touching me wherever they wanted to—stand here, take this off, bend over, don't make a sound, spread yourself for me, hold this inside you, not with your hands.

Of course it would have made me painfully envious if I'd seen anything like that in the theater, but I'd have taken an excruciating blast of jealousy any day over what I actually encountered. After the pinchy pair, I'd seen another couple impersonate some regular old domestic violence down near the stage toward the bottom row of seats. The man ordered the submissive woman he was with to take her blouse off (nudity was allowed), and I could see from her face that she clearly hadn't heard him. If I could see it, I didn't get why he couldn't see it, or if he had, why he'd still yelled in her face and yanked her shirt up over her head as if she'd insulted him somehow with the delay. She looked genuinely sorry, at any rate, and I felt my heart sink, for her and for me. Was I crazy to think I might ever find a sexually dominant partner who'd be nice to me?

Suddenly I felt a nudge on my right shoulder. An older man, perhaps in his sixties, was grinning at me from a couple of seats away.

"You should go down there," he urged, pointing to the stage.

I looked at him, surprised. I could tell that he meant to be jokingly friendly, but it aggravated me. It would never occur to me to poke a stranger and tell him what he should or shouldn't do, whether I knew he was into sexual submission or not. I resented that he had taken me for someone who was open to receiving orders just from the look of me.

"That's not really my thing," I said politely and shook my head, hoping to discourage further interaction.

"Well, what is your thing, missy?"

A lame attempt to make flirty small talk was one thing; calling me *missy* was another. I wanted to tell him my thing was being left alone. And then I thought, *I don't have it in me to be bitchy to an old man right now. Fuck!* I was just so deflated from the whole experience.

"Um." I rolled my eyes around the room, pretending to consider his question. "You know, I'm still sort of new, and I just came here to watch."

I offered another tight smile and heard a man's voice cut across the rows above us.

"Leave her alone, Richard, ya pervert."

The old guy next to me and the man who'd yelled at him chuckled warmly at each other. I turned around to see if I could get a look at the owner of the slightly scratchy, Midwestern-sounding voice.

A man with graying blond hair was smiling at me. He looked to be in his early forties—a dozen or so years older than me—and his pleasant face was almost cute, I thought. I turned back to the demonstration below, grateful to be out of the conversation with old Richard.

"We're not always this boring," a whispering voice came close to my left ear. I turned around, startled. The man who had teased Richard into leaving me alone had moved down a row, and was sitting directly behind me.

"It's . . ." I didn't want to bash the mummy act, but by now I just didn't have the energy to come up with a good lie. Before I could make a stab at diplomacy, he interrupted me with a wave of his hand.

"It takes forever, it's not that sexy-looking, there's not even any pain involved—you don't have to say it, I know it's boring. I just don't want you to be scared off from joining. Some of us are a lot livelier than this, especially at the parties."

I laughed, relaxing a little. Maybe this group wasn't so bad after all; maybe I was still a little defensive in the aftermath of T. The guy behind me seemed easy enough to talk to. And there was something else as well—*there's not even any pain involved*. The words had caused a little chill to run through me.

It had been so long since I'd experienced any kind of pain that felt good. I wondered if this man was skilled at making it feel like something I'd want more of.

"I'm not scared off," I said, and turned around in my seat so I could get a better look. He had blue eyes that crinkled into slivers when he grinned, which he seemed to be doing every time I glanced his way.

"My name's Clark." He reached across the back of my seat and I shifted to shake his hand. He gave me a firm and gentle squeeze before settling back into his chair.

"Nice to meet you. I'm Joan."

"So, you going to join? You can come to our next party if you do—it's in a couple of weeks."

"I don't know really. I've never been to a party like that and I'm not sure I'm ready, honestly." Everything I had done with T had been just the two of us in hotel rooms, and I had been self-conscious enough even then.

"You ever played before, or is this all new to you?"

"Both, I guess. I had a, um, Master"—I still felt weird using the term, but wasn't sure what else to call him—"for about a year and a half, and we did a lot of things together. That ended a few months ago. But I still feel pretty new."

"I'd be happy to help you change that, if you like." It came out more like a half-joking offer of assistance than a smarmy come-on, which made me laugh.

"Thank you, but I'm probably not ready to play publicly," I began. He cut me off.

"I didn't mean just at the party. I meant if you're comfortable coming to my place or having me over, I'd love to play with you."

"How do you know that you'd love to play with me?" I asked, feeling slightly suspicious for the first time.

"I know that you're polite. I know that you're genuinely submissive." He looked at me seriously.

I didn't want to badger him, but I wanted to know why he was so sure of the latter assessment. Was it just because I'd mentioned having a previous dominant partner? How did he know we hadn't broken up because I *wasn't* genuinely submissive, whatever that even meant?

"I know that you're cute—" He crinkled his eyes at me again. "—and I think I'd be a good person for you to play with. You have a lot of anxiety, and we've already established that I'm safe and experienced."

"It's true that I don't get a creepy vibe from you, but just because you haven't attacked me here in public doesn't necessarily prove anything."

Clark laughed without a trace of defensiveness. I knew for sure that I liked him then.

"I have to go, but here's my number." I bent to grab a pen out of my purse. I was afraid if I stayed any longer, I'd end up following Clark home that very day in a rush to finally get some physical relief. "I'm pretty busy through the week, but maybe we could talk sometime next weekend?"

*Could it really be this easy, after all this time?* When I handed Clark the piece of paper with my number on it, he took it with one hand and grasped my wrist softly with the other, circling the width with his thumb and middle fingers.

"You're pretty tiny," he nodded, "but I definitely have something that'll fit you."

I felt my face getting warm, but let my hand stay in his, until he dropped it gently and smiled his goodbye.

On the drive over to Clark's place a few days later, I felt distracted by thoughts of the upcoming meeting. It had taken exactly one phone conversation for me to decide to meet him at his house for the kind of kinky sex I'd been craving ever since things had gone south with T. As my little car chugged and wheezed along the freeway, I wondered what it would be like to feel Clark's large hands around my waist instead of my wrist. Or maybe he'd start by holding my wrists above my head, pushing me face-first up against a wall, and using his other hand to spread my legs? Would he order me calmly to bend over some piece of furniture, like T had the first time we'd met, telling me softly to lift the skirt of my dress so he could look at me, touch me, remove my panties himself?

A large sign registered in my peripheral vision and I realized with a start that I'd come close to missing the exit. Once I'd gotten off, I took an instantly critical stance of Clark's hometown. It seemed to be one charmless duplex or apartment building after another, with desperately unattractive little stores and sprawling gas stations filling in the few gaps. One of Clark's explanations for choosing it had been the low price of his condo, and the built-in privacy it offered for his "private dungeon." By my estimations, he could also have saved whatever money he'd spent on equipment and just considered the drive over torture enough for whomever he played with.

I pulled up in front of his place and leaned into the car's air conditioning vents, hoping to chill my skin before subjecting it to the sweatiness of the air outside. It was hot that day, even back in civilization, so I knew it'd be a scorcher between my car and Clark's front door. I flipped down the visor to take a look in the mirror. I was glad to see that all the time I'd spent on emphasizing my best features that morning hadn't gone to waste—my eyes still looked wide and green, my lips a little plumper than their actual size, and my skin was nearly flawless with the light coat of foundation and powder. I imagined that my shaved, moisturized legs looked creamy white instead of ghostly pale under the short black dress I'd washed and dried the night before, and I felt pretty confident when I rang Clark's doorbell.

As the door swung open, I was treated to a smell not unlike the one I used to encounter when I'd worked at an animal hospital. Stepping into his front room, I realized that, rather than having done even the slightest bit of tidying up, Clark must surely have hired someone to come over and make a mess. I'm not saying that people need to do every last dish and straighten every magazine on the coffee table before I arrive. I do, however, think it's normal new-sex-partner behavior to try and make your living quarters look like a place a person might want to sit or lie down in, and to rid it of any assertive smells that aren't of the pleasant variety. Still, I remained stubbornly optimistic. Maybe the dungeon itself was where he'd concentrated all his cleaning skills.

I took a deep breath and forced myself to exhale slowly, realizing suddenly that I was more nervous about what he might think of me once I was naked than what I thought of his messy front room. I looked to Clark for some sign of how this type of thing was supposed to proceed.

"You want to go upstairs?" he asked. He had dressed casually in a dark blue polo shirt and faded jeans and seemed completely relaxed.

*Thank God,* I thought. "Sure." I forced a smile out of the nearly frozen muscles on my face.

As he led me to the dungeon at the top of the stairs, I felt my fantasies disintegrate at the sight of it, this secret chamber that had been the subject of my daydreams over the last few days. It had been soundproofed, and the windows covered to protect the neighbors from freaky tableaux, but, rather than a dungeon, it felt to me like a closet. Someone's big walk-in closet that had been cleared out except for some miscellaneous dusty stuff that nobody wanted and that the closet owner had been too lazy to take with him. I tried to think kinky sex but instead kept coming up with images of vacuum cleaners and Hefty bags.

I walked over to a rack on one wall that held several whip-like objects and some leather cuffs of varying sizes. I was hoping to disguise the disappointment I felt with a noticeable interest in his equipment.

"Want to see what some of them feel like?" His voice was casual and low behind me.

I turned to face him. "Sure," I said again, feeling hopeful and self-conscious at the same time. I let him steer me to the opposite side of the room, where some kind of homemade, padded bondage rack had been placed up against the wall. He pulled gently on my hips, positioning me in a slightly bent-over shape.

"Okay, we're gonna start with a warm-up." Clark began flogging me lightly with a multistranded whip I hadn't seen or heard him pick up.

His strokes came within a few seconds of each other, and I heard more than felt them; over the thick cotton of my short dress, the leather strands might as well have been landing on someone else's ass for how much impact they were having on me.

Clark stopped for a moment and stepped up behind me.

"Is this okay?" he asked softly, lifting up my dress and tucking the back of it into the waistband of my underwear. I nodded twice and felt myself start to breathe heavier—his nearness and the warmth of his fingers as they grazed my skin were a bit more like what I'd had in mind.

Still, I continued to have to strain to feel any of the strokes as Clark went through a buggy whip, riding crop, and a couple of small paddles. I wondered why he was going so easy—he knew I had some experience. Was I supposed to ask him to do it harder? Or would that be impolite? I didn't know. With T, I'd generally been out of breath and halfway to needing a break five minutes into any of our encounters. I was trying to conjure the right way to phrase a question when I felt Clark's hands in the waistband of my panties again, this time taking my dress back down and smoothing it over my ass.

"That'll do for now," he informed me cheerfully, and patted me gently on the shoulder, ushering me casually back out the dungeon door. He suggested I make myself comfortable in the guest bedroom directly across the hall while he went to make a quick phone call.

"Sorry, it's my brother's birthday today and I wanted to make sure I didn't miss him, with the time difference in Minnesota," he explained about ten minutes later. "How you feeling?" he asked, smiling brightly at me.

"I'm okay," I lied. I noticed that something in Clark's manner suggested that this had not been just a temporary break in the activities. I sat up straighter and tried to keep my voice steady as increasing frustration took hold. "Did I say something, or has something happened that I'm not aware of, 'cause I kind of thought . . ." I looked at him for a clue to what was going on.

"You know what, kiddo, I don't think we're going to do this today. I sense that you're not ready." He sounded like a coach informing an injured player of the sad news that he'd be on the bench for the rest of the season.

"But, uh . . . " I struggled to make sense of what I was hearing. "I thought that's what you invited me over here for?" I was sure at first that this was some misunderstanding. *He thinks I'm not ready, I know I am, surely we can clear this up.*

"I like to feel a connection to the subs I play with. Has it occurred to you that maybe I'd like to feel more between us than just sex? That maybe I'd feel used if we messed around before that connection was established?" He thumped his chest with an open hand.

For half a second, it almost made sense, what he was saying. And then I wondered, *hadn't he known when he invited me that we weren't connected yet? And if a connection was absolutely necessary, wouldn't it have made more sense to attempt to establish it outside of such a sexually charged place as his personal dungeon?*

I sat motionless on his bed then, staring at the textured white wall directly across from me. I wasn't sure what he expected of me now, or what I felt like doing anymore. Leaving in a huff seemed too revealing—hard to argue that there is enough of a connection if you're prepared to bail just because someone won't put out when you want him to. Staying seemed the opposite of anything desirable; the only tolerable activity that I could think of right then was the obliteration of consciousness brought about by nasty sexual acts. I couldn't fathom what I should do next.

"So, what is it you want from me then, if that's not why you talked me into coming over here?" I finally blurted out.

We had gone through a whole ritual of his supplying references, discussing the things I absolutely didn't want to do, and me telling a trusted friend where I was going and when I'd be back. We could have had a more dangerous time meeting up at the local Starbucks, for my money.

Clark chuckled. "Why don't you lie back on the bed and I'll show you?"

I perked up a little at that—maybe this was just some kind of mind game, a test, and he'd be launching into the more enjoyable stuff if I passed? Feeling tentatively hopeful, I eased my way into a flat position on the bed and stared at the cottage-cheese ceiling while Clark picked up one of my hands and then the other, lightly stroking each finger. It did feel kind of nice. It didn't turn me on at all, but it was relaxing, like part of a professional massage or something.

"Okay, now it's your turn," his perky voice interrupted my semi-nap and I opened my eyes halfway.

"Hmm?"

"Now you do me. Here, I'll teach you."

I sat up, stone-faced, and let him show me what he wanted me to do. *I guess this could be considered some kind of sadistic foreplay if I were a glass-is-half-full type of person,* I thought, more perplexed than ever. As Clark stretched out on the bed, I began to do to his fingers what he'd been doing to mine a few moments before. A couple of minutes into the literal hand job, Clark fell fast asleep.

Dropping his hand in stunned silence, I lay down again, getting as many inches away from him as I could while still being on the same bed. His throaty snores felt like little sonic slaps to my face. I couldn't seem to help but take it personally.

I mulled it over, trying to figure out what had gone wrong. *Let's see . . . he invited me here to have kinky sex . . . I showed up groomed, dressed nicely, and in a willing and eager mood . . . he showed me his home-made dungeon . . . and now he's asleep instead of perversioning me.* It seemed like some vital piece of information was missing, but I couldn't locate it no matter how many times I ran over the afternoon's events in my mind.

I sat up again, accepting at last that he simply wasn't going to go back to flogging me or doing anything else I'd fantasized about. I gritted my teeth against the sound of his sleepy cuddling noises when he stirred next to me.

"How you doing, sweet thing?"

I bristled at the endearment and mumbled that I was fine, excusing myself to use the bathroom.

It seems like whenever I'm angry outside of my own home, I find myself locked alone in a bathroom. I think my penchant for sitting on a closed toilet lid and hashing over the shortcomings of others developed in my childhood, when the bathroom was the only room in the house where I could be alone and unquestioned. There was something that soothed me about returning there, even in a strange place. Behind the locked door, seated eye level with the sink, I could let my face fall into the rich scowl I'd been holding back with great effort for the last half hour.

"Hey, you hungry for pizza?" Clark called from the bedroom next door.

"Yeah, that sounds great," I yelled back. I was actually famished by that point. I hadn't eaten a big lunch because I hadn't wanted to have a bloated stomach the first time he saw me naked. Yeah, I was fucking hungry for pizza. I ran my hands under the faucet just to make some kind of bathroom noise and then stepped back into the hall. Clark was leaning against the frame in the doorway to the guest room, waiting.

"You want to drive down there with me or stay here and nap?"

"You know what? I am still kind of tired. If you don't mind, I think I'll just lie down for a little while until you get back."

As soon as I heard Clark's garage door close I surprised myself by starting to cry. As I lay back down on the guest bed, warm tears tickling my hairline, I worried that this fiasco was a sign that I just wasn't going to get to have good kinky sex ever again. I could not for the life of me understand why, but there was no mistaking that it didn't seem to be working out for me. I thought briefly of leaving while Clark was at the pizza place, but the prospect felt somehow even more humiliating than what had already gone down. Or not gone down, to be exact. Why should I have to scurry off like some criminal on the run? *He* was the one who'd been an asshole, not me.

When Clark returned home with two greasy circles of cheese and meat, I had a couple of slices before saying a fake-friendly good-bye. He said he'd call me, and I bit back the urge to spit *why?*

In the weeks following, I tried to go with the idea suggested by a friend, that possibly the universe was simply sparing me from getting involved with someone who wasn't right for me. Maybe everything happens for a reason and for the best, ultimately, and so there was nothing to be upset about. But something about that theory struck me as fishy. I knew so many people who were having sex with partners who weren't right for them. I was the last person who would have invited the powers that be to intervene and save me from the same fate. *Who asked YOU to help?* I felt like yelling at the sky.

One night a little while after our chastity party, Clark called me again, wanting to know when I was coming back to his house.

"Things are kind of hectic right now," I answered noncommittally, and walked the cordless phone into my back hallway. I visualized pitching it into the toilet, at the same time considering how to wrap up our conversation immediately.

"Yeah, for me too. Plus I got dragged out to keep my friend company during her slow shift at the dungeon the other night," Clark offered disjointedly.

I wondered if she was a friend he'd previously deemed *ready* and had the graciousness to fool around with, and raised my middle finger to the phone in the bathroom mirror.

"What do they do there?" I asked casually.

"They do sessions, straight spankings and stuff, no sex. Don't you know what a commercial dungeon is?" he asked.

"I guess not," I said, suddenly interested in what he was telling me.

"Girls get paid to play with strangers. If they don't have experience, they have to start out as submissives. It's part of why most of the subs there aren't any good to play with anymore—they're all dommes in training, they're not even into the sub sessions they do," Clark snorted.

I walked out to the front of my studio apartment and squatted down on the edge of my mattress. "What do these women look like?" I asked, squinting skeptically at what I was hearing.

"All different kinds," he said, "but mostly pretty average. Some of the dommes are pretty hot, but mostly they're just normal-looking girls. Why?"

"So you don't have to look like a model to work there," I mused, getting up to turn on my computer. "Do they have a Web site I could look at?"

"Yeah, it's www.dominionsm.com, but I'm telling you, you don't want to work there," Clark warned suddenly.

"Why not?"

"Because I've seen it ruin several perfectly good submissives. They get lots of clients 'cause they're the real thing, and then all of a sudden they're burnt out and won't even play in their personal lives anymore!" he fumed.

"I already have a job," I said evasively, and decided not to point out that if he really thought I was so "perfectly good," he shouldn't have blue-balled me the day I went to his house. I thanked him for his advice and said good-bye.

As I waited for my prehistoric desktop to go through its laborious connection process, I thought more seriously about the dungeon. I'd been half kidding myself when I asked Clark for the information on it. *Who,* I thought, *would hire a square-looking secretary to do any kind of sex-related work?* But his description made it sound different than I had at first imagined. If other women who didn't look like movie stars made money at it, who's to say I shouldn't check it out?

It seemed ideal, really. Instead of meeting someone from a personals ad or at some other gathering of faux vampires, fey Goths, or passive-aggressive suburbanites, I could meet a well-behaved pervert in a private, chaperoned, and safe place. I suspected that, by this point, I could enjoy being dominated by almost anyone who bathed and had a good attitude, especially since I wouldn't have to be kissing or fucking him. It sounded almost too perfect, to think I would get to satisfy all my cravings without any pressure to decide or explain my further romantic interest in a person, or lack thereof.

My jaw dropped as I scanned the Web site a few minutes later. Clark had been right. With the exception of a couple of the dominatrixes, all of the women pictured were, at best, averagely attractive. I'm no supermodel, but I was at least as cute as most of the women staring back at me from my computer screen. I felt the same rush of dazed excitement I'd had the first time I'd gambled in Reno, when I'd won a five-hundred-dollar jackpot on a slot machine that had just taken my last silver dollar. Within an hour of receiving my initial e-mail, the owner of the dungeon invited me in for an interview. *I have some experience as a submissive,* I'd written, *and I'm prompt and reliable.* Two weeks later I was seated in the plush, cherry-scented waiting room at the dungeon, waiting for my first client to arrive.

## TWO

**"HEY, HOW HEAVY** are you, Marnie?"

Samantha had called out the question from the front desk. I'd been waiting awkwardly in the adjoining lounge area for about half an hour, not making any conversation with her or the other woman I was working with that first Saturday afternoon. Samantha was voluptuous and heavily made-up, and looked to be in her early thirties. Her fantastically large breasts pressed softly against the top seam of her latex bra. She wore matching latex shorts that showcased her textured thighs and broad hips. I wasn't used to women with natural bodies revealing them outside of the locker room at the gym.

I had developed an instant crush on her.

Taylor was the physical opposite of Samantha—tall, not an ounce of fat on her, and, other than a little black eyeliner and some lipstick, her smooth pale skin appeared untouched by man-made improvements. She wore shiny red patent leather boots that flared out like a superhero's when they got to the middle of her long, lean thighs. She must have had on some actual clothes as well, but all I remember from that first day is those amazing boots.

"Um, I think I'm about a hundred and seven pounds right now; I'm not sure because I don't have a scale at home," I began to answer.

"No, I mean how heavy of a *spanking* can you take?" Samantha laughed.

"Oh! I think I can take a pretty heavy hand-spanking," I said, feeling my face redden.

"What time are you gonna come in, Bill?" I heard Samantha say. I looked at Taylor, sitting cross-legged in the opposite chair. She smiled back at me encouragingly.

"Would you happen to know anything about the guy Samantha's talking to? I'm a little nervous today and not sure what to expect," I said.

"Oh yeah, Bill. I've played with him before." She paused. "I started as a sub but now I'm a switch," she confided. "He's just a very regular client who likes straight, over-the-knee hand spanking. He's really good about respecting limits, but you have to remind him about giving a good warm-up. He spanks pretty hard."

"Marnie, I just got you your first session!" Samantha yelled.

"Wow, that's great!" I had actually started to feel a sense of panic well up in my chest, but I didn't want Samantha or Taylor to know this. A man was coming to this place to see me, in order to cause me pain. Erotic pain theoretically, the kind I tended to fantasize about almost constantly, but my rational mind worried about the sound of it, regardless. "Is there anything I should know about him?" I called back.

"Yeah, he's a hard hand-spanker. But it's not that bad—my ass always goes numb a few minutes into it," Samantha assured me.

"*Oo,* not mine!" Taylor said. "Mine just burns the whole time. But Samantha's right, it's not that bad. And he only sees girls for half an hour at a time."

"Well, is it gonna be tolerable or . . . ?" I'd been craving a good spanking for so long now, but the way they were talking about Bill made me wonder if I wasn't in over my head.

"Look," Samantha suddenly barked, "how do you expect to make it here if you can't even handle a simple spanking?"

"I *can* take a simple spanking!" I protested. "I just don't know how to tell if your idea of heavy is the same as mine." I wasn't pleased with the insinuation that I might be a wimp.

"Well, maybe we should show you," Taylor said, and then looked at Samantha, shrugging. "Are you comfortable with that, Marnie? You know you don't have to do anything you don't want to do here. . . ."

Was she kidding me? Was I *comfortable* having one or two cute girls spank me just for the hell of it? I tried to contain my glee and pass myself off as coolly agreeable. "No, totally, that's fine, I'm comfortable with it. If I know what to expect I'll be able to know whether I can take it."

It sounded so pragmatic, I was sure neither of them could tell how turned-on I was. I don't know if they would have been glad or put off by it; I just didn't feel like risking any potential alienation on my first day.

"Okay, come in here," Samantha instructed. "I'll show you what I think of as light, medium, and heavy swats, and you tell me what's okay with you," she said as she pulled me into one of her arms, bending me slightly at the waist so that my face was over her shoulder and my ass stuck out in front of her. "You ready?"

Taylor joined us, standing behind Samantha so that she and I were nearly face to face. "Is this okay with you?" she stage-whispered.

"Uh, yeah, this is definitely okay," I said. "And yes, I'm ready."

"This is light," Samantha informed me, and gave me a quick slap on the seat of the little sundress the owner had suggested I wear for my first shift. "This is medium," she announced, and then spanked me slightly harder. "No, wait, this . . ." She spanked me again, harder this time. " . . this is medium."

"Okay," I agreed.

"Now here's how Bill spanks," she warned, and delivered a sat-isfying amount of sting to the apple of my right cheek.

"Can you do that again?" I asked, "I just want to make sure I understand."

"Sure," she said, all business, and spanked me again. When she let me up, I started laughing.

"No offense, but I can't believe you guys had me worried over *that*."

"Yeah, but with Bill it's not like what I just did. It's more like a machine gun, right, Taylor? No warm-up, no rhythmic pace with breaks and build-up, just *bam-bam-bam-bam-bam!*" she smacked her hands together hard several times.

"That's all right. If you're sure you hit me as hard as he will, I'll be fine. You said he's a nice guy and everything . . ."

"Yeah, he's okay. He'll even come in for a session if he knows one of us is in trouble with rent or something. He's just kind of geeky, that's all. He's the sort of guy who wouldn't mind if Taylor or I walked into your session. He's like family around here. He just," she thought for a moment, "he just thinks of himself as our disciplinarian. He really believes he's *helping* you, straightening you out and stuff."

"Well, I don't know how much straightening will result from it, but he'll definitely be helping me if he shows up," I said.

I wasn't thinking only of the physical release either. I just felt much better knowing that my very first professional session would be with someone who seemed to be thought of as a kind of house mascot. And even if hand-spankings were about the safest kind of SM activity a person could engage in, it was good to know that things weren't likely to get out of control. One of my biggest wor-ries had been that I might get hurt in the wrong way at this job.

As if reading my mind, Taylor looked at me with real concern and said, "If anything ever starts to happen in a session that you're not comfortable with, you can end it immediately if you want. We're all here to back each other up."

"Thanks," I said, nodding, although I had a hard time understanding how that would work. If all went well, there would be other sessions where I'd be alone in a room with a man, perhaps bound, but certainly at a physical disadvantage no matter what. "If that should ever happen, how would I, you know, ever get out if I needed to?"

"There's an intercom in every room if you need to call for help," Samantha explained.

I didn't want to risk being called a coward now, after establishing that I was, at least, not a lightweight, but I still had to ask. "What if I'm, you know, tied up, or have a gag in my mouth?"

They looked quickly at each other. Samantha shrugged. "It really boils down to the fact that if you ever get even a tiny bit of a weird vibe from someone, or if something in your gut tells you not to do the session, you shouldn't do it."

Since these women were still strangers to me, I didn't just take their word for it that Bill was harmless. I decided to use my pre-session interview with him to practice my vibe-getting skills.

"Is there anything we should talk about before we start?" I asked Bill as we sat facing each other in the lounge. We'd been ushered there after his arrival and now the door was shut. Whether someone booked a session with a specific woman or came in and picked someone working the shift, the two of them were supposed to talk for no less than a couple of minutes and no more than a few before starting their session.

"I'm told you can take a pretty good spanking. Is it true?" Bill asked. He looked an awful lot like R. Crumb, minus the hat.

"That's right. And you're mostly into hand-spanking?" I asked.

He nodded. "I heard you came in late today, and I know Hillary wouldn't want you making a habit of it." Hillary was the blonde, buxom, semi-mother-figure who'd hired me. She owned and ran the dungeon, the actual name of which was "The Dominion," after having worked there as a submissive and dominatrix herself for years.

"You should know that she comes to me regularly with any disciplinary problems she has with staff." Bill looked pleased with himself and was apparently trying to impress me with his sternness.

I kept a straight face just barely. Did people really believe this shit or was it actually a campy joke on their part? I had some curiosity myself about certain kinds of role-playing that seemed exciting, but to be talking in normal conversation and then have someone act like he's really taking me in hand and I'm really going to let him?

I had no talent for pretending to believe myself in need of guidance or punishment. Well, truth be told, I had no talent for pretending much of anything. I'd failed Beginning Drama my freshman year of high school. Lucky for me, Bill's own theatrics were enough to satisfy him. He got up and I followed him out to the front desk.

"We're going to go for half an hour," he told Samantha.

"Why don't you take her into the Dean Martin room?" She marked down our starting time in the ledger. "Don't forget, Bill," she turned to look at him, "you need to give her a good warm-up. She hasn't been spanked in a while so start easy, okay?"

"I gotcha," Bill answered, and walked me down the hall to the Dean Martin room.

After closing the door behind us, he sat down immediately on the long bench that ran along one wall and patted his right knee. "Okay, come on, young lady. Let's go."

I hadn't known what to expect, but I really hadn't envisioned such an abrupt beginning. As I moved toward Bill from where I'd stood semi-frozen near the door, he reached out and grasped my left arm, tugging me quickly across his knees, steadying me with his other hand around my waist. I felt a little silly initially, staring down at the shag carpet, wondering if the porn-shop smell was coming from the candles on the shelves or some kind of disinfectant in the adjoining bathroom.

"So you were late today, huh, for your first day of work?" Bill asked.

"Well, I was out kind of late last night and hadn't expected it to feel so early this morning when my alarm went off . . ."

I decided on the spur of the moment to play along out of curiosity. *How can something this contrived possibly turn people on?* I wondered, *or is it me? Am I a wet blanket? Don't even the women's magazines and beer commercials now insist that role-playing is the latest sexy thing? Could I possibly be the squarest person who ever worked in a dungeon?*

Bill lifted my dress, revealing my black thong. Hillary had told me that something "sweet and sort of innocent-looking" would work best for an outer garment, and that thigh-highs, garter belt, and a G-string would be what all the guys were looking for underneath. Bill seemed only to be looking for the best place to bring his hand down. As his right palm landed on the fleshiest part of my right cheek, I gasped in surprise at how little pain I felt.

"Ouch," I offered anyway.

"That's what happens to young ladies who show up late for their first day of work!" he said, and spanked me again. Promptly switching into the mode Taylor and Samantha had warned me about, he began laying fast-paced, fairly hard swats on me nonstop.

I couldn't help myself. I started laughing. I don't know if the corniness of his smug admonition did it, or if it was the sheer absurdity of someone paying to slap my ass like this. I couldn't have stayed in character at that point if I'd wanted to. The fact that Bill let my laughing go unremarked endeared him to me a good deal.

"So, you live around here?" he asked, mid-swat. He paused a second for my answer.

"No, actually I live a little north of here. What about you?"

"I live about a half hour from here, near Marina del Rey. I drive up a lot, trying to keep the girls in line for Hillary," he explained.

"Do you have any cats or dogs at your house?" I asked, for no particular reason, and made a mental note to chat Bill's ear off if we ever did a session that actually hurt. Since his spanking method made it hard to hear anything over the repeated sound of his palm meeting my flesh, he was forced to stop anytime he wanted to catch what I was saying.

"I have a cat," he said.

"I have two, and they're both pretty crazy. Is yours nutty, too?"

And that was pretty much it. In between the small talk with

harmless, quirky Bill, he spanked me. We talked about whether I would go back to school, if he liked his job, what had made me apply at the dungeon, and our cats.

Before too long, there was an abrupt sound of loud static and then a woman's voice could be heard saying "Knock! knock!" This was the house code for "time's up." I wasn't sure yet how the intercom actually worked. Did I have to get up and press a button, or could they hear me if I simply answered back? I stuttered an "Okay" in the direction the voice had come from and removed myself slowly from Bill's lap.

"Well, that was just great, young lady. You certainly have a lovely bottom for spanking." Bill beamed at me.

"Thank you, and thank you for such a fun first session."

I felt a little awkward, not yet knowing the right way to end these things. Was I supposed to curtsy and leave, or what, exactly? Fortunately, Bill took the lead by asking for permission to hug me and then gave me a clumsy embrace before opening the door.

If Bill's had been the only appointment booked that afternoon for me, I might have felt discouraged. But after he walked me out to the front desk, another man headed back with me to where I'd just been. Hillary, who had relieved Samantha at the desk, told me his name was Robert. He was around my age, stood about a foot taller than me, and looked pretty well built under his button-down shirt and loose-fitting slacks. His thin lips split over slightly bucked teeth when he smiled to introduce himself, and it was hard to tell if his eyes were sad or if he was just really tired. He was somehow cuter than the sum of his parts might have suggested, and it made me nervous as we passed through the small kitchen area and what I thought of as the tool shed (an open closet space where most of the equipment hung or was stacked).

The Dean Martin was the smallest room for sessioning in the house. Pictures of Dean Martin and his friends decorated the walls, and, in general, the room was decked out to feel like some fancy Rat Packer's den. The spanking horse in the far corner—a piece of furniture that people could straddle or sit on for prime corporal punishment positions—made it harder to picture Frank and Dean sitting around with their cigars and brandy snifters, but otherwise the room was pretty straight-looking. As Robert politely motioned me into the only comfortable chair in the room—an under-stuffed armchair covered in some metallic-green vinyl—I noticed for the first time the magazine and hairbrush that lay atop the small table next to me. *WHAP!* exclaimed the headline of the publication. "*Women who administer punishment,*" read the type underneath. I felt the familiar flush of excitement that such materials always caused me; it was like a tiny space heater had been turned on in my stomach.

Robert sat across from me on the narrow bondage table, smiling as he folded his hands together in front of him, and I hoped my involuntary reaction to the magazine didn't show on my face. Even in this environment, it still caused me some embarrassment. What was business as usual for everyone else was still like winning the sexual lottery for me, and I felt somehow unsophisticated because of it.

"Hillary tells me you're new," Robert finally addressed me.

"Yeah, I just got out of my first session."

"Did you enjoy it?" I noticed he had a way of holding my gaze with his own while he smiled and talked, without it seeming like one of those cheesy *look into my eyes* maneuvers. Already I hoped this interview would end with us deciding to have a session.

"It was fun," I nodded. "Just some spanking, pretty simple and easy."

"Great. Can I ask you, do you prefer sessions like that or are you into other things too?"

"Well, I like a lot of stuff, actually. Over-the-knee spanking *is* one of my favorite things. But I like nipple-clamps too, some bondage, maybe flogging. I mostly just want to play with someone I'm comfortable being around, and try whatever they're into. The only thing I don't really do is humiliation."

"That's good. I'm not into that either, and I can't really relate to subs who are. It's not my thing." It was the best thing he could have said about it, from my point of view, and I hoped even more for a trip upstairs to another play-room with him. "Why don't I tell you a little bit about my own style?" he asked.

I nodded for him to go on.

"I consider myself a sensual sadist, meaning I only want to cause erotic pain to an extent that feels really good to the person I'm doing it with. I'm not into hurting anyone in a real way. I just like to use lots of different sensations, including pleasurable pain, to heighten my partner's experience. Does that sound like something you'd like?"

Did it ever. I couldn't believe I was about to head into my second session of the day. And he said he wanted to go for a full hour, which meant a whopping eighty dollars for me. I could buy a week's worth of groceries and have money left over for the gas bill with this hour of so-called work.

Robert held the door open and then followed me back up to the front desk. He told Hillary that he wanted to have an hour-long session with me, with the option to extend if we both wanted to. Hillary told us that one of the big, plush rooms upstairs, known as the Lair, was open. It had a thick shag carpet like the Dean Martin, and was decorated in pretty much leopard-print everything. It was the most comfortable of the four rooms. Across the hall from the Dean Martin downstairs was the "Vault," where floors, walls, and furniture were all made of cold stainless steel, and next to the "Lair" upstairs was a room called the Rock, for reasons I still don't understand. It was a large space with black rubber floors and black leather everything else, including a faux-black-leather toilet seat in the bathroom.

Robert picked out some floggers, cuffs, and a candle, and got a few cubes of ice before leading me toward the front door, which opened out into a small, enclosed courtyard and to the stairs for the upper rooms. I wondered the same thing, walking up that staircase in front of Robert for the first time, that I would wonder every time I ascended with someone to the comfort and danger of the rooms above—*Does my ass look good moving this way?* I wanted every moment of every session to reinforce the new image

I was forming of myself: sexy, glamorous, different from merely pretty girls. I wanted to come across like one of the va-va-voom broads from whatever decade it was where round hips were appreciated as the luxury they truly are.

Up in the room, Robert had me sit on the leopard-print bench while he readied the space. He dimmed the lights and lit candles, then put on a CD of his own. Low, mellow-sounding techno music came through the speakers in each corner of the room. Robert grabbed a couple of maroon-colored towels from the adjoining private bathroom and spread one of them in the middle of the plush red carpet. He walked back over to me and, putting his hands on my upper arms, drew me up to face him.

"Close your eyes," he told me softly, and I did. "While you're with me, you're to address me as 'Master.' Is that understood?"

"Yes, Master," I answered, feeling once more swamped in hokeyness but trying to keep an open mind. I hoped this one affectation was merely a quirk and not representative of his general style.

"That's good," he praised my response, stroking my shoulders. He paused to clasp my forearms with his warm hands. "I want you to kneel—I'll help you down if you can't do it alone with your eyes closed."

"Thank you, Master. That would be helpful." I let him take my hands to guide me. Kneeling in front of him, I felt a hand cup each side of my head, softly stroking my hair in half circles. I prayed he wouldn't let his thumbs fall forward to massage my temples. I hated it when anyone's fingers got near my eyebrows. But there was no way he could know that, and his thumbs were about to rest on my painstakingly-secured arches when I jerked my head involuntarily away. "I'm sorry, sir. I have a thing about having my face touched."

He pulled his hands out from my head abruptly. "I'm sorry," he began, but I interrupted him.

"No, no, it's okay. I just didn't think to mention it beforehand. It's not a big deal," I assured him. I liked that he was sorry, though. I hadn't wanted him to feel bad about it, but it was a good sign that it mattered to him to have done something I was uncomfortable with, even unintentionally.

"Is it okay to touch your hair, or is that off-limits too?"

"That's okay, thank you. I like having my hair touched, actually. It relaxes me." He went back to running his fingers over the surface of my hair, sometimes brushing it back a little from my face, but mostly just stroking the length of it the way my Aunt Sue used to do when I was little. I started to feel not exactly drowsy, but not entirely alert either.

After what seemed like a couple of minutes, he walked away. I could hear him doing things, but with my eyes still closed I couldn't make out what he was up to. It occurred to me how nice it was not to be worried about it. After the first time I'd met my former dominant partner, T, in person, all pauses and preparations were cause for anxiety, and justifiably so, most of the time.

"I'd like you to get up now. You may open your eyes," he told me.

I did, and he offered a hand to help me up off the floor. Standing, I was about a head shorter than he. I watched his chest rise and fall as his fingers went to the straps of my dress and pushed them off my shoulders. Using the lowered straps as handles, he pulled the top part of my dress down to my waist, where it rested snugly over my hips. He reached around as if to hug me, found the clasp of my bra with his hands, and let my padded, pushup C cups fall to the floor between us.

"Beautiful," he murmured, taking my now-erect nipples between each thumb and forefinger. He squeezed them gently for a moment, then used the backs of his knuckles and the rest of his hands to caress the sides of my breasts.

"*Mm,*" I said, when his fingertips moved to the curves underneath, back to the swelling on the sides, and up again to my nipples, this time pinching them harder. He let his hands drop to my waist, feeling my width there as if measuring, then slid his hands into the part of my dress that was still on. Gently he worked the material down over my hips, past my thighs, and held the dress for me to step out of when he reached my ankles. I stood in my shoes, thigh-high stockings, and a G-string, feeling somehow fully dressed. With the lowered lights and his compliments, I felt like my semi-nakedness was an outfit of its own that I'd put on.

"I'd like you to lie down on the towel there, on your back, face up," Robert spoke softly.

"Yes, Master," I said, and let myself down onto the towel.

"Close your eyes," Robert said, and I heard his shoes scuffing the carpet away from me again.

A moment later he was back and I heard a match being struck against its box. I jerked involuntarily, and hoped he hadn't seen; burning is one kind of pain that I'm not interested in. I knew he wasn't going to burn me—the match was for a candle I could already smell since he'd lit it—but not being able to see gave me an irrational sense of personal flammability.

"I'm scared right now," I blurted out. "I'm kind of afraid of fire."

"I didn't know that," he said without judgement. "Would you rather not do this part?"

"No, it's okay. I like candle wax. I just felt afraid for a second. Thanks for being nice about it," I said, calm again.

"You're welcome," he said, and I could hear the smile in his voice.

I was aware of the effect my openness had on men, especially perverts—they generally found it endearing and thought I was cute. I very much wanted Robert, and any other good clients, to find me so. More than the validation of it, I was still preoccupied with how bizarre and exciting it was to know that money was virtually piling up outside the door for every minute I spent enjoying myself.

"You ready?" Robert asked me quietly.

"Yes, Master," I answered. Through my closed lids I could make out a brightness that hovered above my midsection. As it moved toward my face, I grabbed my thumbs in clenched fists and held my breath. As the first drop of liquid warmth landed close to, but not exactly on, my right nipple, I made a small noise of surprise. My hands opened flat and I laughed softly when it registered that the wax hadn't hurt at all, had in fact felt more like a kiss than anything.

Robert was holding the candle almost as high as his own chin, standing above me, so that the wax had time enough to cool on the way down.

"You liked that?" he teased me, and I nodded, still smiling.

I waited for the next drop to fall, and cried out when a tiny stream of ice water fell onto my left breast instead. I hadn't realized he'd been holding and melting an ice cube in his other hand.

"Oh my God, that's so cold," I said, shivering.

An instant later three more drops of wax, this time carrying a tiny sting of heat, splashed onto the same area where the water had fallen. He lowered the candle further and spilled another small puddle onto my stomach, taking away the chill completely. "Thank you," I said, "that feels nice."

"My pleasure," Robert said, and poured the melted-ice water onto the triangle of my G-string.

I gasped, then laughed, and heard Robert laugh quietly as well. I willed my body to remain still as the different sensations began raining down on my skin more rapidly. Warm on my upper thigh, icy on the delicate skin covering the tops of my feet, hot and cold simultaneously between my legs, this time lower than where the first droplets had fallen. I didn't realize how loudly I was breathing until I heard a muffled noise and realized it was Robert talking to me.

"I'm sorry, Master, I didn't hear you," I said.

"I was just murmuring in pleasure over the way your skin turns a lovely shade of pink with just the slightest stimulation. It makes me curious to see what color it would turn if you were across my lap, receiving a different kind of stimulation," he told me.

"Hm," I said, feeling shy and a little embarrassed, as I always did, about how excited the idea of it made me.

I have spent a fair amount of time trying to figure out what's up with this spanking fetish I have—where it comes from, what about it exactly is such a turn-on, why I identify being spanked as a good feeling instead of a neutral or unpleasant one. I really have no idea. The only clear thing to me is that the thought of it can create a feeling inside me as if all the blood in my body is suddenly being drained from every extremity and redirected straight to my sexual center.

"KNOCK! KNOCK!" Hillary boomed over the intercom. Robert snapped his head toward the wall where the screech came from, and yelled back.

"EXTEND!"

He looked back at me, post-declaration, and raised an eyebrow to confirm my agreement.

I smiled up at him, still barely believing that this was happening to me. It was a heady feeling to be with someone who had more authority with the boss than it seemed other clients did. I knew Hillary would have buzzed back to confirm with me if this hadn't been the case.

Robert helped me up and gently dried me off where the ice water had left me damp. His hand, covered in the towel, pressed into my wet G-string several times, blotting as much of the water as possible from the darkened material.

"Your hand is warm," I said into his shoulder as I leaned against him for support.

"Let's see what else of yours it can warm up."

I let Robert take my hand and lead me to the leopard-skin bench that was pushed up against one of the walls. It was long enough that I could get across his lap, which I did promptly, resting my arms on it in front of me with the length of my legs and feet resting on the other side of him. It was a comfortable way to spend an extended period of time. I rested my head in the space between my arms as Robert started to slap my cheeks softly to warm me up.

Soon, Robert began to increase the tempo and intensity of his spanking. He had a great technique. He knew exactly the right spot where the sensations of a thud and a sting came together to produce a satisfying jolt between my legs. Somewhere in the middle of the fleshiest part of each cheek was an area that felt internally connected to both my G-spot and my clitoris. I couldn't tell you the mechanics of any of it; I'm just saying that a genuinely good spanking, even a hard one, never registers as real pain for me.

When my partner knows what he or she is doing, it causes a sensation unlike either pleasure or pain, yet somehow indivisible from each.

I could not tell how much time was passing, but after a long stretch where the only sounds were Robert's hands landing on me and my satisfied moans, he began slowing the pace, alternating between rubbing and spanking me. After a little while, I felt his hand falling harder and harder on my skin, instead of the backing off and the rubbing that had been going on a minute before. I began to squirm, thinking I might be reaching some sort of threshold, and I felt his other hand tighten around my waist to hold me still. This sent shock waves of even greater excitement through my body, making the burning in my cheeks momentarily more tolerable.

"*Please,*" I begged finally, unable to recall my safe word in that moment, but not really wanting to use it anyway.

I didn't want him to stop entirely, which he would have done if I'd given the safe-word signal, but I didn't think I could take an indefinite amount of this kind of intensity either. Reflexively, I tried to rotate my hips on his lap, and again he gripped me tighter, preventing me from moving at all this time. Increasing the pace and sting just a fraction more, he held me against his body for another full minute. This time, his clasp caused something new to happen. Something akin to pleasure began to radiate outwards from the pit of my stomach up into my chest and down into the throbbing between my legs. I gasped into the cool leather of the bench beneath me, begging him one last time, but not for anything I could put my finger on.

He stopped, finally, and I stayed immobilized across his knees even when he no longer had such a firm hold of me. Both of his hands went to my ass, sometimes rubbing with his palms, sometimes running his fingertips over especially tender areas. I stifled the fuck-drunk urge to blurt out that I loved him.

"*Jesus!*" I finally breathed, as Robert helped me up to stand unsteadily in front of him.

"That was great," he said, and began rubbing my bare shoulders. "Would you like to lie down for a minute?"

"Yes, thank you," I said. He joined me, fully clothed, on the towels still laid out beneath us. He inched closer to me, until we were shoulder to shoulder staring at the ceiling like it was a star-filled sky.

"You don't have to tell me, but I'm curious where you got the name Marnie."

"Are you sure you want to know? It might freak you out . . ." I hesitated.

"Now I definitely want to hear it. And I'm not that easy to freak out, for the record."

"Okay. I'm not comfortable with the whole fake name thing in the first place, and I definitely didn't feel like choosing something cute or forced—sexy or whatever."

"I can understand that, after knowing you a couple of hours now," Robert said, turning his head a little.

"Right," I paused. "So the only thing that came to mind for me was a fake name that someone else had used a long time ago. Marnie K. Reeves was the alias that Patricia Krenwinkel used when she got arrested for the Manson murders." I took a breath. "Plus, I don't know, something about that girl that always made me a little sad. I mean, it was horrible what they did. But she got called ugly a lot during the trial, and it seemed unnecessarily mean. It's not like her looks were what killed those people."

"That's true," Robert nodded, and I was relieved that anything I'd said had made sense to him.

"I guess she stuck in my head because I knew what it was like to get called ugly a lot at that age." I shrugged.

"Now that I don't believe." He shook his head.

"Hold it." I put up my hand to shush him; I hadn't been trying to play the I'm-ugly game, fishing for compliments. "Let's just say it was before I *blossomed*."

He laughed, and then turned to me, rising up on one elbow. "Don't take this the wrong way . . ." he began, and I braced myself.

"There's something about you that's different. You don't have that hard look that a lot of women have in this business."

"Well, it *is* my first day," I joked, relaxing. "Give me a minute."

"That's what I mean," he chuckled. "You're sort of more of a real person, in some ways. I don't know . . ."

Naturally, I liked the idea that I was special, but I cringed at the pro-sub-with-a-heart-of-gold cliché. I felt like there was probably a reason a lot of women were guarded and hard in this or any sex-related business. I wasn't sure that it was smart to put value on any praise that set me apart from them. I had a murky sense of how it made me vulnerable, not better, no matter what a client might say.

Robert helped me clean the equipment we'd used. We blew out the candles together. As we walked back down to the front desk where he could settle up and I could get signed out, I thought about what an amazing day it had been. Two acceptable men, all that money, and more sexual release than I had felt in years in just a few hours' time. I didn't know if I could stand to wait a whole week before I came back.

# THREE

**THESE ARE SLAVE'S** *wages,* I grumbled to myself without irony.

It was my first Monday back at my job after my afternoon at the Dominion. *Fifteen bucks an hour to wear sweat-inducing polyester pantsuits and stand watch over a cold, metal desk that reeks of inactivity.* It was only eight-thirty in the morning, and already I felt like a caged animal. A *guilty* caged animal. I had an absurdly easy job, and it was an almost obscene lack of gratitude that I now felt for it. I worked for a funny, nice man who didn't even need a secretary, but had wanted one just to keep up appearances. He was a vice president at a nonprofit that provided a variety of services for the blind. I was required to answer about four phone calls on a busy day, and type a letter about once a week. Up to this point, it had been the cushiest, best-paying job I'd ever had.

But it was also true after that first Saturday shift that I could make a lot more doing a lot less. I could not undo what I now knew about kinky sex work; could not make myself return to my previous state of contentment. Wrong or right, I would never again view my desk job as anything other than the wrong kind of pain in my ass. I had to find a way to work as a professional submissive full time. The world did not need one more cranky secretary, of that I was certain.

I spent that Monday calculating and re-calculating how many hours of sessions I'd need a week to cover my monthly budget. It seemed to me that I might be able to make the transition to full time at the dungeon pretty quickly, but, to be sure, I quizzed Hillary the next Saturday before we opened.

"Generally, Marnie, it takes about six months for girls to build up enough regulars to make a pretty steady living at this," she told me.

Six *months?* I didn't feel like I could last another six *days* at the office. "Wow. Isn't there anything I could do to speed up the process a little?"

"Well, you could certainly get more sessions if you were here more often, but it's still a matter of the clients getting to know you, people finding out that you're available. It takes a little time to get established, that's all." The phone rang and she reached for the receiver.

"Dominion, how may I help you?" After listening for a moment, Hillary responded by naming everyone on shift at the time, noting who was submissive, who was dominant, and who switched, doing both. After another minute, she thanked the caller and hung up.

"That's a guy who's coming in for a sub right there. See, you're already on your way!"

As on the previous Saturday, I was the only submissive on shift when I got there, and I liked it that way. I went to the Dean Martin to change into one of my new dresses.

I'd gone to a local shop on Melrose called Retail Slut after work one night. I'd been sure that I felt the judgemental eyes of the two young salesgirls, sizing me up as clearly more *retail* than believable *slut*. No thanks to their skeptical expressions, I'd still decided on a couple of dresses that could have passed for nudity if I'd had leopard-print skin, and then picked up my first adult lipstick from the MAC store in the Beverly Center. The last lipstick I'd owned had been some frosty pink business that I was sure would get me laid my senior year in high school, and that I had promptly tossed in the garbage when graduation day had come and gone, my virginity still intact.

After I was finished changing, I went back up front to stash my purse and clothes in the employee closet. Hillary was gone and a lanky, short-haired brunette was in her place behind the front desk. Taylor was in one of the lobby chairs, lacing up another pair of beautiful black thigh-high boots.

"Hey, Marnie." Taylor looked up and smiled at me. "This is Vanessa, another domme who works here," she nodded toward the woman at the desk.

"Nice to meet you," we said at the same time, and then laughed politely.

I gave Vanessa and Taylor an awkward wave as I moved into the television room. I still didn't know what to make of the other women on staff here. What did the subs and dommes generally think of each other, and did they all feel as uncomfortable as I did about competing for clients' business?

Plopping down in one of the comfy chairs in front of the television, I picked up a magazine instead of the remote control. *Whips and Chains,* it announced in bold red letters across the top. A pretty young blonde woman graced the cover in full fetish gear—black leather corset, lacy blue-and-black bra and panties, fishnet stockings and impossibly high spiked heels. Her hands were on her hips as she stared, unsmiling, directly into the camera. *A Slave's Punishment!, Hardcore S/M Pictorials!, Hundreds of Domina Listings!* barked the headlines on the cover. I flipped to the back and was surprised to see a half-page, full-color ad for the Dominion. Seeing it was an added thrill for me; it made me wonder how many other publications, small or large, were running ads for our dungeon rooms and showing staffers' pictures.

Then another advertisement caught my eye, this one a little smaller and in black and white, for what looked like a commercial dungeon similar to ours. Suddenly I realized we might not have a corner on the market, and I felt a stab of insecurity about the prospects of there being enough clients to go around. Maybe my first shift had been a fluke. Maybe there would never be enough money to support me full time after all, no matter how long I gave it.

"How many places like this are there?" I walked back into the lobby and held the open magazine out in front of me.

"What kind of places?" Vanessa looked up from a book with lined pages and some kind of inked entries.

"Like this one."

"Darling, there aren't any other places like ours!" she winked.

"There's an ad right here for one," I pointed at the troubling text for the other place I'd just discovered. "And what about all these other people?" I tapped the varying announcements that were lined up in neat columns on the page opposite the Dominion's ad. There were quite a number of listings for Mistress-This and Goddess-That, covering the Los Angeles and Orange County areas.

"*That,*" Vanessa pointed a sharp red fingernail at the other dungeon's ad, "is not a place like ours. It's a shit hole where the pimp-owner makes mistresses take their clothes off in session and tries to shortchange everybody's pay whenever he thinks they're too stoned to notice."

"Oh," I said.

"Those others," Vanessa took the magazine gently from my hands. "Let's see—" She scanned the page and flipped to another one. "Some of these women are escorts pretending to be pro dommes, and some are real dommes who work independently. You can pretty much tell by what they say in their ads. Look." She pointed again. "This one says she's into sensual domination, allows full-body worship, some massage. That's a dead giveaway she's a hooker. *Full-body* means he can go down on her, and *massage* means she'll jerk him off at the end. Can you picture a real domi-nant woman doing any of that?"

I didn't know what to say. T had wanted me to go down on

him all the time, and had loved touching me to try and make me come. I looked at Vanessa with raised eyebrows and a shrug.

"But this one here—" She pointed to another ad. "—this one is a real domme. That's Mistress Catherine. She works downtown, has her own great space, and has been around for a long time."

*She must have started when she was twelve, then,* I thought to myself, eyeing the youthful face of the woman in the ad. It would be months before I would find out that "a long time" in this business meant anything over two years.

Vanessa handed the magazine back to me and I found the page where the ads started and skimmed through them. I was relieved to find no other "dungeons" per se, but was curious about something else now. "I don't see any ads for submissive women working on their own."

"Of course you don't," Vanessa sniffed.

"There aren't any pro subs working independently, Marnie," Taylor spoke up, finished with her boots.

"Why not?"

"It'd be much too dangerous for a submissive! How could a girl protect herself if she were meeting strangers out on her own like that?" Vanessa frowned at me.

"But don't people like Catherine meet strangers on their own?"

"That's different. They're in *charge* of the sessions they do. A poor sub girl would be totally at the mercy of God knows what kinds of psychos!"

On the surface, her argument seemed logical to me, but then I thought, *how could it be any more dangerous than working here?* It seemed to me that, either way, I would end up alone in a room with a man I didn't know who wanted to hurt me in one way or another. I mean, I guessed there was something to be said for having a bunch of potential crime-scene witnesses around, but my gut sense already told me that most men who sought out these kinds of sessions weren't interested in genuinely harming anyone.

As I wondered about sharing these conclusions with Vanessa and Taylor, the loud sound of someone's arrival at the front door put an end to the discussion. After checking his bona fides over the intercom, Vanessa buzzed in a tall, broad-shouldered, darkly good-looking fellow who couldn't have been more than twenty-five.

"Hello," he said, his eyes shifting between the three of us. Vanessa immediately took charge.

"Hello, and what can we do for you?" her tone was formal, but her smile was slightly warmer.

"Well," the young man said, clasping his hands together, "I was hoping to see about a tickling session today."

"Okay? So tell us, are you looking for a submissive or a mistress?" Vanessa fixed him with a prying gaze.

"A submissive, hopefully," he answered politely.

"Well, our Marnie is a submissive, hopefully," Vanessa smirked playfully over at me, and I caught the man's gaze for a moment before looking away. He had a huge, delighted grin on his face. I had been standing between the desk and where Taylor sat while we'd all been talking. I wasn't sure if he'd been looking past me at her.

"What's your name, please?" Vanessa asked.

"Daniel."

"Marnie, would you like to take Daniel to the Dean Martin for an interview?"

I felt my neck and face start to color. *What if he wasn't smiling at me, and now Vanessa's put him on the spot?*

"Um, would you like to . . . ?" I looked at Daniel, trying for an expression that conveyed a polite and non-pushy openness, to cut down on any awkwardness in case he wanted to back out.

"I'd love to," he grinned more broadly, and this time, for sure, he was looking directly at me.

"I feel like I should tell you up front," I said as soon as he'd closed the door behind us, "that I'm not really a ticklish person, nor would I be very good at faking it." I hoped he wouldn't be irritated that I'd wasted his time by doing the interview.

"Really?" he smiled at me, unfazed. "I could've sworn you looked like someone who'd be a lot of fun to tickle."

"Well, thank you," I said, not even sure why I took this as a compliment, "and I'm sorry to be the one to break it to you that I really wouldn't be. You seem nice, for what it's worth. I wish I *were* the type of person who'd be good for you." I shrugged apologetically.

"That's sweet," Daniel said, seemingly unmoved by the discouraging news. "But honestly, I'd like to do this anyway. You're *very* cute. I'd like to session with you, please," he finished. I felt my face growing warm again.

"Thank you—"

"Oh my God, I can't believe you're blushing," he laughed. "I haven't seen anyone blush in years. How cute is *that?*" he said, embarrassing me and fondling my ego at the same time. I tried to will my skin back to its natural color, and began again.

"I worry that I'd disappoint you, is all."

"I understand that. Consider me fairly warned. If it works, it works, and if not, no harm done. I really just want to be alone with you, now. I'm not even sure I care about the tickling part. Unless you're just not interested in playing with me at all?"

He looked at me with his cute young face, wide brown eyes pretending to fear rejection. Even knowing it was some kind of a game, I didn't have it in me to blow him off. It was the guy-like-him-finding-me-so-cute part that killed me. I'd wanted guys like him to find me cute since puberty had wrecked me at age thirteen. Even after I'd started looking good again as an adult, living in L.A. had made it almost irrelevant. The standards of beauty here were such that any woman without a tan, fake boobs, and a twenty-two inch waist was rendered all but invisible.

"No, I am. I mean, yes I would," I stuttered. "Be interested in a session with you."

I couldn't help thinking how strange it was that I'd be getting paid to be touched by someone who might have ignored me for free if we'd been out at a club. It wouldn't be the last time, by a long shot, that I would have the sensation of having been deposited into someone else's body, someone else's life. Sometimes I had to check the mirror to make sure that, in fact, I wasn't having some kind of "Freaky Friday" experience. Was there some really gorgeous woman somewhere who was now getting used to feeling average in a super-square life?

"Do you know if the Lair is open right now?" Daniel asked me.

"I think all the rooms were open, at least when we came back here five minutes ago."

"Great. Let's go grab it before anyone else does!" he smiled, but I thought for the first time that I saw something resembling nervousness. That relaxed me a little bit, to be able to see him as vulnerable too, in his apparent hope that it would go well.

By the time I reached Vanessa, one of Taylor's regulars had already come in and they'd gone up to the Lair for a two-hour session. I broke the news to Daniel when he joined me in the front—he'd taken a detour to the clients' restroom before making his way back to the lobby.

"The Rock Room is open, though," I told him, "and it's somewhat similar to the Lair, I think?" I looked to Vanessa for verification.

"Yes, darling, it's quite lovely, I think you'll find it more than sufficient," she smiled at both of us.

"Do we need anything else before we go up?" I asked Daniel.

"Hm. What about some cuffs? Are you comfortable with that?"

"Sure." I led him back to the tool shed where we found two pairs of leather cuffs lined with fake fur for my wrists and ankles, and Daniel picked up a couple of pieces of rope as well.

I hadn't really gotten a good look at the Rock Room before then. Hillary had asked one of the other subs to show me all the rooms on the day I'd interviewed, but there hadn't been any time to explore. As I stepped into the all-black room with Daniel, I had to leave the door open just to find the light switch. All the windows were covered. I couldn't see past the end of my nose if I moved more than a few inches from where the light streamed into the doorway from the little sunroof in the hall. When I found the switch, it was already on. This was apparently as bright as the Rock Room was going to get.

As I made my way across the room, I heard what sounded like a door lock being engaged, even though we were supposed to leave everything unlocked here. I turned back to Daniel as he followed me into the center of the rectangular room, and then thought better of saying anything. What difference did it make, anyway? It's not like an unlocked door was magically easier for me to get to if things went awry in a session, and the doorknob turned from the inside even when locked to the outside. I didn't want to risk blowing the mood with him by seeming critical.

"So, which do you like?" Daniel motioned with either hand to the two bondage beds in the room. One had been manufactured to look like an old-fashioned stretching rack. It took up nearly one-half of the far side of the room, and wasn't as wide as the other bed, which filled the large nook next to the bathroom closer to where we stood. I pointed to the nearer one and went over to set the cuffs down.

The bed was all black leather, with a black-lacquered wooden frame, and several metal eyehooks had been screwed in at equal intervals around the perimeter. Daniel approached me from behind and then his hands were on my shoulders, massaging warmth into my chilled skin. All the rooms seemed to be kept at the same icy temperature. I guessed it was to help the dominatrixes keep cool as they cracked whips and kicked crotches in latex catsuits. I wondered if I should invest in a little space heater for my own sessions.

"Mmm," I said, letting my neck roll slightly back as his hands relaxed me.

"Why don't you take this off while I get set up?" he fingered the spaghetti straps of my dress. I slid out of the clingy sheath and waited silently while he tied pieces of rope onto four of the hooks, spaced approximately the distance between my own arms and legs. He patted the table and I sat down, scooting into the middle where he'd indicated.

"Lie down, Marnie" he said.

"Would you like me face-down or face-up, sir?" I asked. It felt a little weird to address a kid his age as sir, but youngster didn't seem right either.

"Face-up is good to start with." He smiled again, and I stretched out on my back as he began placing the cuffs on my ankles.

"Sir, I forgot to ask—is it okay if we say *mercy* is the safe word? I know it's not likely that I'll need to use it, but—"

"Sure, that's fine. *Mercy* it is. Are these good?" he asked, tugging on an ankle and a wrist cuff with each hand.

"They're fine, thank you, very comfortable," I answered, thinking how I'd wished all my working life for a career where lying down was part of the job description.

I closed my eyes as his fingers spread more warmth over my calves, the tops of my thighs, my ribs, my breasts. He ran his fingertips like feathers down the sides of my abdomen, then swirled them in light circles under my arms. I opened my eyes to look at him, to see whether he seemed to care that I wasn't giggling. He didn't look mad as I watched him pondering where to try and tickle me next, his gaze traveling the length of my body.

He poked the first three fingers on each hand into either side of my ribs then. That kind of touch had indeed felt like tickling to me in other situations, but this time it felt only like a jab. A jab that turned me on for no reason I could understand, and I surprised us both by moaning and lifting my upper body closer to his hands.

"You liked that?" Daniel asked, trying to sound flirtatious, but unable to totally conceal his confusion at my reaction.

"I guess so," I said uncertainly. "I don't know why, though—it kind of hurt," I finished.

"In a good way, or . . . ?" Daniel asked, and it did seem to matter to him at the time.

I didn't know how to answer him. I wasn't sure I wanted to encourage more of the same. I knew it wasn't considered very safe to receive any kind of pain to areas of the body that weren't well-padded in fat. Rib cages are generally off limits.

"Um," I began, not sure how I was going to finish, and was interrupted by some more poking, this time not quite as hard, although still enough to hurt. Again I arched my back and breathed heavily through my mouth as his fingertips prodded bone and skin.

"I'm sorry," I gasped, "I don't know why I'm having this reaction."

In my confusion, I was afraid that, somehow, my being turned on would be an actual letdown for a person who was looking solely for the types of screams and giggling that normally accompany a tickling experience.

"Nothing to be sorry about," Daniel grunted, and climbed up on the bed to straddle my hips.

The cool leather of the tops of his shoes rested on my outer thighs as his fingers went back to tormenting my torso. He was smiling above me now, and something in his expression unnerved me. His sizable and very hard erection pressed into my pubic bone at the same time as his poking became more intense and unfocused.

"Um, uh," I was having a hard time translating the sensations and my response to them, but I had begun to feel worried about what we were doing. "Um, mercy!" I suddenly yelled, having finally felt a jab that was only painful instead of a blurry pleasure.

Daniel stopped his strange tickling technique and let his hands massage the places on my body that now felt red and tender.

"Mm," I said, pushing my body up into his hands, using that movement as a chance to clandestinely tug at my wrists and ankles, to get a sense of how helpless I really was. It felt like I could probably pull my wrists through the soft fur inside the cuffs if I needed to, but the ankles didn't seem to be budging. As I sunk flat again onto the bed, Daniel's hand caressed its way down between my legs. It felt good, but I knew it wasn't something we were allowed to do.

"I'm sorry," I said with true regret, "but we're not allowed to be touched down there."

"Okay, sorry," Daniel said, and pulled his hand away reluctantly. "I gotta do *something* with them," he joked lamely. He pressed his hips more firmly into mine as he went back to thrusting his fingers into my sides.

"*Ouch!*" I said, squirming underneath him, aroused once more without understanding why.

He slid his hand back down between my legs.

I almost said nothing. By this point, despite my bewildered enjoyment of his odd assault on my ribs, it was nice to take a break anyway. "I'm sorry, sir, I really can't do that. I could get in trouble."

I felt instinctively that it was better to blame the house, to stay on friendly terms with him.

"*Aw,*" he said, screwing his face up to mimic pronounced concern. He kept his hand in place on top of my G-string and rubbed me more vigorously then. "I'm not really touching you, I'm just checking to see if you're wet or not." He grinned at me but without humor now, his face only inches above my own.

How to explain . . .

Under other circumstances, I would have loved for someone as cute as him to touch me like that. But his bitchy disregard made him grotesque in that moment, and sent me into a flat-out rage. I jerked on my cuffs and pulled my hips away from the center of the table where his hand was on me.

"You have to stop now," I said tightly, no longer even attempting to sound conciliatory about the refusal.

It seemed to work at first—until the removal of his hand from my crotch turned into the placement of that same hand around my throat. He grasped firmly without squeezing, and it had the strangest externally soothing effect on me. I went completely limp, and searched his face for what, if anything, I should most be afraid of.

"I told you, I was just checking," he said through gritted teeth.

We stared at each other for a minute, and I could tell then that all he wanted was for me to be soft again. It didn't even bother me in that moment to have to placate him, instead of telling him off. It felt like the only practical thing to do, and I was relieved to have such a clear idea of how to help myself.

"Okay," I said and fixed an open expression on my face as I continued to look into his eyes. "I just got scared," I told him, the truth of which allowed me to say it with real sincerity. He seemed to snap out of something, then.

"I don't want you to be scared," he said, and sounded like he meant it. He took his hand away and sat back on his heels.

Suddenly, I felt this weird sadness between us. It had been sweet such a short time ago, and then—this. I could tell from the look on his face that he felt shitty about what he'd just done. *As well he should,* I thought, but felt my anger slipping into pained confusion. I had clearly been turned on. He thought that meant I wanted to be touched. How many times would he have heard or read that women into dominance and submission had fantasies of being "forced" to submit to pleasure without responsibility? How does a person on either side even begin to translate those reckless images into a responsible reality?

"KNOCK! KNOCK!" Daniel jumped off the bed completely at the sound of Hillary's voice.

"Thank you," I said to the intercom, and watched Daniel closely as he began untying me without comment. He rubbed my left wrist after pulling it free, then seemingly thought better of handling me any further. After releasing the last cuff on my ankle, he turned back to me on his way to the door and waved stiffly.

"Well, take care."

"You, too," I answered lamely, and waited to get up until he'd closed the door behind him.

I exhaled loudly at the ceiling, feeling the adrenaline I'd had to ignore when he'd still been with me. I felt something else then as well, something that made me even more uncomfortable than what had just happened with Daniel. *It's just a reflex, it doesn't mean anything about anything,* I told myself emphatically. But I really had no idea what it might or might not mean—that even in the midst of my fury at Daniel, my body had still been aroused by being restrained and touched without permission.

After gathering up the equipment and wiping down the table with alcohol and paper towels, I opened the door to head back downstairs, and then closed it again. *What am I going to say to them about it? Should I even say* anything? I flashed on what Vanessa had said about pro subs not being able to work independently, and worried that she or Hillary might decide I couldn't handle working here, either. *I should keep quiet. There's nothing anyone can do about it, anyway.*

I didn't get any other sessions that shift, and spent the remaining few hours watching television and trying to make sense of the day.

Had I really been in danger, or had I overreacted? And if there had been a real threat, and I had been turned on even in the midst of it, I couldn't help but wonder if my response made me more of a danger to myself than any man could ever be. I knew I had been really pissed off, not some porno-queen version of sexed-up helpless victim, but I still understood so little about my kinky urges. It felt impossible to tell whether they came from the part of me that just loved having good sexual encounters, or if there was a darker drive being stimulated, a drive I did not romanticize or wish to nurture.

As I was getting ready for bed later that night, something odd caught my eye in the mirror. I thought for a moment that perhaps some kind of dye had rubbed off on me at the dungeon. I looked more closely, and saw fingertip-sized spots of black, as well as robin's-egg blue, dotted along the length of my rib cage. I patted the bruises gingerly to see whether they hurt or only looked bad, and then dropped my hands nervously. Pressing them, I'd felt myself on the bed again with Daniel and had that familiar mixture of resentment and confused arousal. I knew I hadn't felt that way at all with Robert or Bill the Saturday before. What we'd done together had felt *normal* to me. I didn't know what other word to use for it. I knew also that these feelings I was having now mimicked pretty closely the way I'd felt throughout the entire relationship I'd had with T. I wondered which experience of S/M was the exception, and which was the rule.

# FOUR

CLIENTS OFTEN ASKED about the first time I realized I had a fixation on both spanking and erotic dominance and submission. The truth is, unlike some other kinksters, I could not remember a "first time" or a defining moment that flipped an internal switch for me. As far as I know, I always felt like I do now. What *did* stand out was the first time I understood that this feeling I got in my stomach around kinky stuff was connected to sex.

At age fourteen, I decided to try something I'd read about in Judy Blume books, despite the popular rumor at the time that masturbation either made you a lesbian or proved you already were one. One night during my eighth-grade year, an image formed seemingly out of nowhere in my mind's eye as I pressed and stroked underneath my bedcovers.

I saw the boy I had a crush on spanking me.

Whatever blood had not already migrated underneath my right hand rushed hotly to my face and neck in the pitch-darkness of my bedroom. Humiliated, I forced the picture out of my mind. A minute later, as I'd been trying to think of this same boy kissing me, the spanking scene re-invaded. And this time, I noted something besides my embarrassment—the image of being over this boy's knee accomplished a kind of excitement that made the work of my fingers nearly irrelevant. I fought it off a second time, now worried I was beyond the bounds of extreme mental illness, never mind lesbianism. But I did not take my hand out from beneath my covers. When I saw myself a third time, ass in the air over Willie's lap, I gave up. I let the image have its way with me, shutting my eyes tight against whatever it might mean.

Afraid of a recurrence, I lived in frustrated self-abstinence for the next few years. A girl named Mallory helped break my dry spell at age sixteen, passing around a bodice-ripper she'd picked up at the local drug store.

"This is so sexy! Oh my God, you guys have to read it," she'd announced in the girls' bathroom, holding the book out to my friend at thigh level, as if it were an incendiary device that might detonate at a higher altitude.

"What's it about?" I asked. I was heavily into both Stephen King and true crime by then, and hesitated to take my mind off the distraction of terror and bloody death for a mere Danielle Steele rip-off. At sixteen I had bad skin, worse hair, a tragically misguided sense of fashion, and—needless to say—my virginity. By that point, I needed something more than raven-haired beauties and throbbing manhoods to keep suicide off the top of my to-do list.

"Just read it," Mallory growled quietly, waving us away as she disappeared into the halls.

I not only read it, I tore through it. A sexy Arab prince kidnaps a beautiful young woman and brings her to his luxury tent in the desert. When he's not at work in his sandy kingdom, he's banging the hell out of her in a way that makes her forget, at least during the banging, that she's mad at him. He tries to win her over with good sex and witty repartee, but she insists on trying to escape anyway. When she brandishes a pair of sewing scissors—after all he's

THE PLEASURE'S ALL MINE

done for her—it's the final straw. He knocks them from her hand and pulls her over his knee. By the time he's done spanking her, they both know she's in love with him.

*How dare he?* I raged inside. *How dare the author, how dare the publishers, how dare the world at large pretend that this is what makes women happy?* Just because it made *me* ache with longing didn't mean it was realistic or right. Yet a smaller voice inside me did find some comfort amidst the indignity of this kind of propaganda. Mallory, too, had found it sexy, I remembered, and, indeed, the fact of its publication in the first place proved to me that I must not be the only person in the world who felt this way. And there were now at least some options for the future—if I could somehow grow up pretty enough to be the object of a handsome kidnapper's attention, I might be able to get the spanking and sex that I now thought about on a daily basis.

Still un-abducted years later, I tried to get my first couple of boyfriends to help, but their attempts to humor me were always awkward and frustrating at best. None of my fantasies had involved being slapped like a horse getting the giddy-up signal while doing it doggy style, and I was still too uptight about my yearnings in the first place to go into any helpful detail about what would have worked. It was to their credit that all these guys were up for trying. But their failures merely served to accentuate my despair over ever getting what I wanted.

Relief appeared one day during my junior year of college. I'd just gotten a university e-mail account, and had taken to visiting the computer science building after class each afternoon. I didn't have a computer of my own, and the basement of the computer lab had a dozen or so antiquated machines set up for student use.

One spring afternoon, I received an e-mail from a friend of a friend I'd never met, asking me if I'd ever been tied up. This type of thing was not as out of the blue as it sounds. At that time, I was a latecomer to a sputteringly social computer-geek community that had loosely formed a few years earlier. The guys in the group, or geek boys, as we called them, were habitual in their random come-ons to newcomer women. Claiming the mantle of kink for oneself was a common enough ploy among them. It didn't necessarily mean anything except that the person saying it wanted to be thought of as a sexual dynamo. Even knowing it was quite possibly an affectation, I answered my e-mailer with as much controlled enthusiasm as I could muster. *No, I haven't been tied up,* I typed back, *but I've always wanted to be.*

*Meet me in the woods behind the computer lab in fifteen minutes* came the immediate reply. He had to be kidding—there were bugs out there. And though he may have been a friend of a friend, this was Santa Cruz, California, a town that had only recently shaken off the distinction of having the highest percentage of serial killers per capita. Still, the invitation was irresistible. Ten minutes into the waiting period, I headed toward the back door of the building, trying to develop an air of reserve to camouflage my blind hope.

Minutes later, I stood before him in a little clearing he'd led me to. He sat on a fallen log, watching me with a smile in his eyes but nowhere else on his face. I had reflexively followed his first order and taken off my T-shirt and bra without comment.

"Stand in front of that middle tree there, and lift your arms over your head," his voice came again, low and confident.

As I had walked out the back of the building to meet him, I had merely hoped for someone who didn't gross me out physically. His name was Tim, and I had been extremely relieved by the first sight of his cute face and fit body. His brown hair was not quite thick enough anymore to grow as long and wild as he seemed to be aiming for, but it still framed his slightly dangerous-looking face in a flattering way. His skin was pale, more due to time spent indoors than as a result of his natural coloring, and his smooth white hands looked capable of anything I might desire.

Immediately after lifting my arms, I heard a noise. My first thought was: *Is a deer going to freak out if he sees this?* I worried that what we were doing out in nature was somehow tantamount to a form of spiritual littering. I cut my eyes away from Tim and was alarmed to see a flash of color, chest-high, many yards away, moving in our direction through the foliage.

"There's someone coming," I said in a panicked voice, and crossed my arms over my bare chest.

"Stay exactly as you are," Tim ordered, his tone polite yet insistent. I stared at him open-mouthed, and then raised my arms again uncertainly.

"What if he sees me?"

"Probably it'll make his day. Don't move."

Rational thought tried to force its way into my mind, but the jolts of electric excitement traveling the length of my upstretched body refused to be overridden. *Don't move.* No matter who came around that corner, I knew I would remain still. I could not mess up the opportunity to hear Tim say more things like that to me.

Holding my breath, I heard more clearly the sound of crackling leaves and the whoosh of movement through the stillness outside our little circle. When a clear outline of a blue T-shirt bobbed into view a few feet from where I stood, I clenched my eyes shut and waited for catastrophe. Over the roaring of blood in my ears, I heard twigs snapping directly in front of me, and opened my eyes to see who was about to make a citizen's arrest for this public lewdness.

"You were very good. That pleased me a great deal," Tim said, running his long index fingers from the hollow of my throat out to the tips of each nipple. The jogger had passed us by without incident; whether he'd seen us or not, I'd never know. Goose bumps shivered their way to the surface of my entire body in the warmth of that spring afternoon.

"Turn around," he ordered softly. Keeping my hands raised, I swiveled until my back was toward him.

"Bend over. You may put your arms down now."

"Thank you," I said sincerely. My arms had been starting to ache. I leaned forward with my hands at my sides, and studied the close-up view of the ground in front of me. I'd heard there were wolf spiders in these parts, and was nervous about pitching face-first into a nest of sharp fangs and eight hairy legs.

Tim stood close behind me, his crotch pressed lightly against the seat of my jeans. I took deep, sometimes shuddering breaths as the pads of his fingers brushed coolness across both of my shoulder blades, thumbs meeting on my spine to guide his palms down the back of my rib cage. His fingertips curled into the waistband of my jeans and gave a slight tug.

"I'd like you to pull these down so I can further examine you."

I hadn't shaved recently, as I hadn't foreseen any nudity in my immediate future.

"I . . . feel like . . . I'm not ready for that today," I stuttered.

Tim was quiet for a moment. "That's fine, but next time I expect you to be ready to do everything I tell you to do. Understood?"

I nodded, relieved. After allowing me to stand up again and get dressed, he hugged me quickly, but made no mention of when next time might be.

It happened four days later. I had begun shaving my legs daily in order to be ready for our next meeting. Each afternoon when my classes were done, I made my way into the basement of the computer lab. It wasn't until the end of the week, Friday afternoon, that Tim's e-mail came through. He wrote that I had ten minutes to meet him at the edge of the woods, and if I got there after he did, I'd be punished for lateness.

I headed quickly to the woods. As I got within sight of our little meeting place, I saw Tim already waiting, and anxious confusion set in.

*I know it hasn't been ten minutes, so I can't be late. Will he be mad at me anyway?*

He wasn't smiling as I got closer, but he didn't look angry either. It was something else.

*Ah, this is a game—he planned to beat me here all along.* The idea aroused me.

He had me walk ahead of him, and although we were on a visible dirt trail, he still gave me directions about where to turn. His voice steered me back into the small clearing from the other day, and again he took a seat on the large log that rested like a bench on the pine needles and scattered leaves.

"Take off all of your clothes."

I stood in front of him, nerves and joy combining inside me to generate a grin that I tried to suppress, fearing it would make me look silly. I removed my clothes as quickly and gracefully as I could.

"Now. We had an agreement that you wouldn't keep me waiting. And yet you did. Do you know what that means?" Tim's eyes teased me when I looked up from my neatly folded pile of clothes.

"Not exactly." I hesitated, although I hoped that I did.

"It means I have to punish you. Do you agree to that?"

"If . . . well . . . yes, okay," I finished nervously. I couldn't shake the paranoia that there was something irredeemably wrong in admitting out loud that I was into this stuff, even to someone else who clearly shared my interests.

"Come over here." He reached out and pulled me closer by my hips. We faced each other, he on the log, me not much taller even as I stood. His hands closed around my wrists, and I didn't know if it was my veins or his fingers that thumped a pulse through the surface of my skin. "I'm going to spank you now," he said softly, and I started to hyperventilate a little. "Hey." He let go of my wrists and squeezed my upper arms gently. "Are you okay with this?"

"I'm . . . it's just . . ." I couldn't seem to breathe deeply enough. "I think I'm a little nervous. I've never done this before."

"It's okay," he said, now smiling. "I'll take it easy."

But I wasn't afraid that it would hurt too much or that he would go too hard. I was afraid of what I would sound like, look like, act like, once I was doing the thing that made me the most excited of anything else I could imagine.

"Come over to this side, and lay across my lap," Tim guided me to the right of him. He held my waist as I folded myself over him. "You can hold onto my legs if you want."

I held onto him for balance, and for proof that this was really happening, not another of my daydreams. When he ran a hand over the curves of my cheeks, letting the edge of his thumb trail down the split between them, I dropped my shoulders and let my chin rest on the side of his knee.

"Are you ready?" His left hand gripped my rib cage firmly.

"Yes," I said, aiming for more of a purr but hearing what sounded like a croak as my voice box wrestled fear and euphoria.

I think it'd be most accurate to say that Tim gave me my first "patting" that day, rather than anything that technically resembled a spanking. His pace and the weight of his hand as he let it fall were careful and soft, just as he'd promised.

*How does a person get a guy to break a promise like that?* I worried silently. Maybe next time I'd have a chance to convey my sturdiness and he'd kick things up a notch.

After about five minutes, he helped me to my feet and offered another stiff embrace. "I expect an e-mail from you tonight, detailing your thoughts and reactions to what we've done so far," he instructed, before walking me silently back to the Computer Science building.

I sat down to write him immediately, grateful for the chance to tell someone, anyone, how exciting it had been, and how much more I was ready for. I told him how I'd had these fantasies for as far back as I could remember, and that I'd never felt as excited with anyone before as I had with him. I liked regular sex a lot, but it had never left me so uncomfortably, perpetually aroused as that afternoon with Tim had. I wrote that I couldn't wait to learn more about what it meant to be a submissive and masochist—as he'd told me I was, in an e-mail sent right after our first meeting in the woods. And I thanked him for being so much fun, and so nice to me.

I received his reply after my last class on Monday. He was going to have to cool things down for a while, he said, take a break, as his girlfriend was having a hard time with their open relationship all of a sudden. He was sorry, but he loved her and wanted to make it work between them.

After the initial shock, I decided that none of it was true. I was convinced that he was reacting solely to my eagerness—that I'd liked it too much, wanted more of it too badly for him not to feel like I'd stolen the thrill of the chase away from him or something. I realized too late that his instruction to be open with him about my reactions was actually a call for e-mail porn—not the outpouring of raw hope I'd sent off to him in fevered anticipation.

The next day, I burned every piece of kinky literature and spanking porn that I owned. I'd told one friend about my trips to the woods; when she asked for an update later that week, I claimed to have lost interest in him. It would be five years before I'd try anything like it again.

Through no fault of Tim's, school went downhill for me from there. I took a pre-existing self-destructive streak and ran with it, until my love for pot and all things pill-shaped had morphed into a run-of-the-mill heroin habit by the time I was twenty-five. When my parents offered to pay for a hospital stay late one summer afternoon, I figured what the hell. I was dying of boredom, among other things, and rehab sounded like an interesting diversion to me.

When I was a little over a year sober, I found myself not much more entertained than I had been back in my heroin daze. Firmly rooted in a $5.15 an hour job selling newspapers and magazines on a corner near my apartment, I thought if this was what the counselors had meant by a new freedom and a new happiness, I'd like to see about getting my old shitty depression back. In a seemingly unrelated incident around the time I was reaching my breaking point, my housemate at the time inherited a Stone Age computer from a friend. I had a twang of nostalgia for all the cute, non-kinky computer geeks I'd messed around with after Tim, and promptly splurged on an Internet account.

Surfing the Web did indeed turn out to be a more interesting waste of time than what I'd been doing. On one of my first afternoons online, I came across a message board that claimed to be a place to discuss feminism. Considering the number of anti-feminist posts that had gravitated to it, I don't know why I was so surprised to see this one among them:

*Ladies, stop lying to yourselves. Admit you want it. Visit www.spankingnet.com.*

Believing it to be someone's idea of subversive humor, I resolved to ignore it at first. I had paranoid visions of some tracking system that kept a record of how many "feminists" were clandestinely taking the bait, for the purposes of a huge AHA! at some future point in time. Although I dreaded being the bad apple that poisons the reputation of the whole group, I lasted only a few hours before I had to return to the computer and look up the Web site.

The site was not only real, it was better than any other real thing I had encountered in a long time. It was a place for the spanking-obsessed to put up personal ads and talk to each other live in chat rooms. With jittery hands, I typed a description of myself and posted it on the Web site, and by that evening, I had received more private messages in my kinky in-box than I had time to scan through before my housemate came home and needed the phone line.

Before pure glee could sink in, I had a bout of nervousness about what I'd posted. In addition to stating I was very new to the whole bondage and discipline scene and looking for a decent, unattached person to explore with, I'd said I weighed one hundred ten pounds and had perfect 34C breasts. In actuality, I was closer to one twenty at the time, and my left breast was a tiny bit bigger than my right one. I had dread-filled visions of finally meeting someone, only to see his face fall before my eyes as he realized I'd oversold myself online. That evening, after my housemate went to bed and I had time to check my messages at a leisurely pace, it became instantly clear that my left breast was the least of my worries.

It was as if the Renaissance Faire nerds had invaded *Hustler* magazine. I know this is judgemental, but I personally can't get it up for people who address me as "M'lady." Worse, these Little Lord Fauntleroys offered poorly written descriptions of everything they wanted to do to me—without so much as an initial "nice to meet you"—leaving me with visions of disembodied tongues shoving themselves rudely toward places they had not yet been invited. I resisted the urge to send out a mass reply consisting solely of the word *Ick*. On a positive note, it was a relief in a way, because all of my own anxiety about whether I'd be able to shed a few final pounds disappeared completely in the face of people who faked British accents in cyberspace.

Thus, I was startled when I read the profile of a man who invited me into a private chat one afternoon not long after. His onscreen name was "T," and while he didn't say anything especially intriguing in his profile, the sheer absence of any kind of clownish posturing was fairly stunning to me by that point. The only problem was that he'd checked "attached" in his marital status section.

*So, was that a mistake or are you actually with someone?* I typed to him that first day. This may sound unbelievably naive, but I didn't get why someone who openly admitted to having a partner would be contacting me. I thought most guys would try to hide being attached if they were on the prowl to cheat, or at least complain that it was a miserable situation that they would be getting out of any minute now.

*No, it wasn't a mistake,* T typed back.

*Well, are you married to this person?* I asked.

*Yes,* he wrote without elaborating.

*Are you in love with her?*

*Very much so, yes.*

By this point I was both confused and angry. Why did the only non-spastic man I'd communicated with so far on this contraption have to wave himself in my face tauntingly if he wasn't available? *Fine, you're sadistic, but this is a little out of bounds even for kink,* I thought.

*Why are you writing to me, then?* I typed.

*I'm looking for a submissive. I particularly enjoy training novices, which your profile says you are; and I liked that you were clearly intelligent and polite.*

I paused for a moment, and then typed *thank you* automatically, proving his point. *I just don't want to be messing around with someone else's husband, that's all. I would feel guilty about it, plus I don't like to share.*

*Understood. So you know, my wife is aware of my search for a dominant/submissive relationship outside of our marriage. We have an arrangement, which allows both for my consideration for her feelings and for her awareness that I seek submissives to train.*

*I'm happy for you and your wife, but I don't want to be with a married man.*

I was irritated now and would have had the urge to slam down a receiver if we'd been talking on the phone instead of online. How dare he think I'd settle for a fraction of someone else's man? How dare he think I wanted so little for myself, arrangement or no arrangement with his wife?

*Okay,* he typed. *If you'd like, I would still be interested in mentoring you to whatever degree you'd be comfortable with.*

*What exactly would that mean, for you to mentor me?*

*Well, it means that instead of being completely adrift in this new situation, you'd have someone to answer your questions, someone who wasn't trying to get anything from you.*

My irritation of moments before disappeared, and, in its place, I felt the beginnings of what I thought would be a safe, and distant, crush. He was here to help me, and as a guy of forty-five, who'd been in the scene almost as long as I'd been alive, he undoubtedly had information that I needed. When he offered to call me that day so we could talk without the lag of typing time, I agreed. When he informed me that I was to call him "sir" and follow whatever instructions he gave me during our actual conversation, I was doubly happy. It seemed I would get to have the safety of a purely platonic involvement, while still experiencing some of the rituals of dominance and submission that I'd already found stimulating. I logged off and sank into the beat-up couch next to the telephone in our living room. When the phone jingled loudly, I made myself wait until the third ring to pick up.

"Hello?"

"Hello, Joan." His voice had an almost whispery quality.

"Hello, sir." I tried to think of what to say next. What would be good kinky-stranger etiquette? Do I launch into my questions, or wait for him to guide the conversation?

"Tell me, Joan, do you have a wooden ruler in your apartment?"

Thank God he stepped in to take the initiative. I realized I was suddenly unable to think of a single question anyway.

"I know I don't have one, but my housemate might. I can go look."

"Do that now," he said gently, and the receiver slipped out of my hand to land noisily on the wooden tabletop.

"Sorry, sir," I snatched it back up and breathed into the phone. "I'll be right back." A minute later, I was seated again. "I found a ruler, sir, but it's three-sided and plastic, not wooden."

"Even better." I could hear the smile in his voice, and purpose-fully refused to think about where this might be going.

It was one handy skill I'd learned in rehab—how to fend off sheer terror of the unknown by focusing exactly on what's going on in any particular moment. *We are just talking. I am just sitting in my living room. Thin, vertical lines of sunlight are shining through the blinds onto our ugly brown carpet.*

"I'd like you to lie down with your back on the couch, and lift and spread your legs so that you have access to the backs and insides of your thighs."

"Okay, sir, I'm in that position." I rearranged myself, scooting some pillows out of the way, and ran through the litany in my mind. *I'm lying down. I'm holding a phone receiver to my ear. Nothing bad is happening.*

"Good. Now I want you to use the ruler on yourself, first on the back of each thigh, then on the insides, ten strokes at a time, and I want you to count out loud for me."

Hearing his instructions, I realized I had never before been so aroused and ashamed at the same time, even back in eighth grade when I'd first fantasized about this. What kind of person sat alone in her living room and beat herself with a ruler while talking on the phone? What if the neighbors heard, and worse, what if they understood what the sounds meant? And yet there was never any question in my mind that I would do it. Already the sound of his voice in my ear felt like a physical touch to me, like his hands were on my body, mostly around my rib cage of all things, pressing my heart and lungs together so that breath, pulse, and longing all became one blended bodily function in response to his calm orders.

"Does it matter which side I start on?" It felt like a silly question as soon as I asked it, a lame attempt to stall and ask for some kind of reassurance at the same time.

"No, it doesn't matter, but why don't you start with your right side? And it needs to be hard enough for me to hear it." It didn't seem as if he thought I was being silly. If anything, I thought I detected a note of genuine warmth in his response, and I wondered if it was just an attempt to put me at ease, or something he really felt.

"Yes, sir," I said, and then, "One."

"I couldn't really hear that," he interrupted me evenly. "Please begin again."

"One," I gasped as I brought one side of the ruler down on the back of my right thigh with as much momentum as my short arm and the position of my body would allow. Before the full sting of it could take hold, his voice interceded.

"That was much better," he sounded like he was smiling again, and the redness on my white leg felt only warm then, not painful. By the time I had finished all forty strokes, I thought either I must have an unusually weak arm, or an unusually high tolerance for pain. I'd tried really hard to make it hurt, but mostly all it had done was make my body throb in a different location altogether from where the ruler was landing.

"That was wonderful. I'm very pleased, Joan."

I thanked him, and wondered why his simple words of approval made me feel simultaneously so happy and so horrified. I did not like to think of myself as someone who sought validation from men, and yet here I was, feeling like a cat who'd been scratched behind the ears just because a guy I didn't know was "pleased" with me. Beyond that, I wasn't even totally convinced he meant it. He could be anyone. He could be laughing at me right now, or taping this for some humiliating purpose in the future, for all I knew.

"Tell me how you're feeling right now." Apparently he was not done bossing me around. I wanted to hang up the phone then, not ever talk to him again. Who was he to pry into my feelings, anyway?

I'd done what he'd wanted me to do, why did he need to know how attached I already was to the idea of submitting to him?

"I'm okay," I said, more to myself than him. *I'm still okay. This is okay.* And then he did laugh, but not at me.

"You don't sound too sure, although it hadn't occurred to me that you *wouldn't* be, quite frankly," he chuckled softly as he spoke.

*Is it okay to tell a stranger the truth, or is that a socially awkward thing to do?* I wondered silently. *It couldn't be any weirder than what I just did, could it?*

"*Ugh,* I don't know," I began. "This is exciting for me, and I'm afraid that makes me some kind of freak. I'm also afraid you'll think I'm weird for it, and not talk to me after this." I exhaled loudly, relieved that at least it was out there.

"Let me get this straight—you're worried that I'm going to reject you for enjoying the things I like doing with you?" he asked seriously.

"I know that sounds strange." I started to explain, and he cut me off.

"That's okay, I just wanted to make sure I understood what you were saying. Let me ask you something, and I'm not meaning this in a teasing way, but is it your experience that that's normal human behavior when you've done something you enjoy with another person?"

"I don't know, really."

I stumbled for the right way to say what I didn't want him to know: that the last person who'd seemed to enjoy dominating me had also appeared to find me repellent afterwards, and had left me with a fear that it was the very nature and depth of my urges that would put people off thereafter. But there was no way to really backpedal from it now, so I told him, with as little detail as possible and admitting fully only to the fact that Tim had hurt my feelings and left me wary of taking any of this seriously.

"But you don't have a choice about that," he said reasonably.

"What do you mean?"

"If you were capable of *not* taking your feelings and desires seriously, we wouldn't be having this conversation. You'd be feeling happily detached right now, and that would be that."

"Then as my mentor, can you help me learn how to do that?" I asked, only half joking. He roared on the other end of the line.

"That's something I liked about you from the start. Even in reading your profile, it was clear you had a sense of humor. But no, I can't help you feel any of this less intensely." He paused. "I can tell you though, that of the things that could potentially make me uncomfortable with you, your excitement isn't one of them. I'm sorry to hear you had such a hurtful experience before; it sounds like the guy was a jerk."

I didn't realize how hunched up and tense I'd been until his simple words made my shoulders drop down to their normal position. I stretched my neck, rolling my head forward and to each side in the couch cushions, wondering what it was that people were supposed to talk about after an exchange like this.

"Tell me, are you still wet right now?"

*Wow! That's* so *not where I would've gone with it myself.* I told him I didn't know.

When he told me to check with my right hand, it turned out that my body was indeed processing what was happening on its own. He asked then if I would like his permission to come. I thanked him but said I'd pass. I'd never done *that* over the phone either, and somehow it felt even more personal to me than what we'd done with the ruler.

"In that case, I rescind the offer." Before I could thank him for his understanding, he went on. "Now it's a direct order. You *will* come for me on the phone today. Are you lying on your back?"

That was sort of the last straw for me, in terms of my resistance to messing around with someone else's husband. He wasn't going to leave his wife for me, so she wasn't going to get hurt, and I had a little less fear now about getting my feelings hurt as well. Last I checked, there was no surplus of men around who were both good at being bossy in a sexy way and even more interested in my orgasms than I was. I came quickly, and loudly, as he listened quietly on the other end of the line.

The next day I sent him an e-mail.

> *Dear Sir,*
> *I wanted to tell you that I thought of you today when I was out. I*
> *was wearing a skirt when I went to the store, and it wasn't until it*
> *rode up during the drive home that I saw the marks. I checked in the*
> *mirror when I got home—the backs and insides of my thighs are blue,*
> *purple, and yellow where I used the ruler. It scared me at first, because*
> *I associate bruises with injuries. But they're shaped funny, like but-*
> *terflies with their wings spread, and now I'm sort of fixated on them.*
> *Am I going to stay this preoccupied with you and with this kind of*
> *stuff permanently? It's making me feel sort of retarded in the rest of*
> *my life.*
> *Sincerely,*
> *Joan*

By the time he wrote back to me two days later, I was convinced I had said too much, and I steeled myself for rejection as I went to open his e-mailed reply.

> *Dear Joan,*
> *I was very pleased to get your note. Yes, you might stay somewhat*
> *focused on what we do together for a little while to come, but even-*
> *tually the novelty will wear off and you'll be able to think of other*
> *things again as well. I wish I were there to enjoy those beautiful but-*
> *terflies. Maybe some day soon.*
> *Warmly,*
> *T*

When he offered to send me money soon after, so I could get a hotel room near where he lived, I accepted eagerly. I didn't feel like we needed to meet first at some public place, or that I should have a friend tag along to chaperone outside the door until we knew for certain he wasn't a well-disguised maniac. I could tell from his voice and the things he said that he wasn't dangerous. Plus, for reasons I didn't really understand, I liked being a little scared. Later I would wonder whether it was that particular preference of mine or his unconditional acceptance of me in our first phone conversation that kept me going to those hotel rooms long after the butterflies had vanished and what we were doing left me more shaken than stirred.

# FIVE

**"DO YOU MIND** my asking about your first relationship?"

A man named Phil was tying me to a straight-backed chair with the soft rope we'd picked out together from the tool shed. It was my fourth shift at the dungeon, and Phil was my first session of the day. I had told him in our interview that I'd only had one "real-life" experience with a dominant sadist prior to my job at the dungeon.

"No, sir, I don't mind," I said, which actually wasn't true. "There's not that much to say, though. We weren't right for each other, but I learned a lot from him."

I hoped to dull his interest with my bland response. It wasn't that I minded his curiosity. I just didn't like thinking about what had happened with T, not any part of it. Even the good times were unbearable to think about now, more painful in a way than the bad. At least thinking about the crappy parts never made me ache for the way his skin smelled, on those occasions when he had let me face him and be close enough to take it in.

Phil wound one length of the rope twice around my left ankle, slipping two large fingers inside the loop to make sure it wasn't too tight against my skin, and then pulled it a few times around the leg of the chair. While there was nothing about being tied up in intricate ways that technically turned me on, I liked bondage sessions anyway. Even when the ropes were tightened in a manner meant to relay interesting sensations, real pain was never involved. I could sit or lie there, with nothing expected of me, as the person dominating me worked away for long stretches of time. Really, I could recommend it to anyone who had an aversion to actual work.

"What made you feel you weren't right for each other?"

I stared at the top of Phil's blond-gray head as he knelt in front of me, and watched the muscles in his broad shoulders move under his button-down blue shirt while he continued his work with the ropes, the chair, and my ankles. While I took a second to think about my answer, he glanced up at me and offered an encouraging smile. He looked to be about fifty or so, although his moderately tanned skin made it hard to tell whether it was time or the sun that had made the cute little wrinkles around his mouth and eyes.

"Mostly, it was that he wanted a slave," I finally answered, "someone who would take anything and everything from her master, and I'm just not built that way."

This wasn't entirely true either. T hadn't ever insisted on the kinky lifestyler's version of "slavery" with me, nor had I even wholly rejected the idea of it myself. There had been, and were still, times when I wanted nothing more than to feel like I really belonged to someone. But I couldn't think of how else to avoid the specifics; ascribing our breakup to differing levels of interest seemed a way to say the issues hadn't been anyone's fault.

"So you see yourself as more of a masochist than a sub?"

Phil finished the knot he was working on and picked up another piece of rope to use on my upper body.

"Not . . . well . . . I think I don't really know what I am yet," I finally admitted.

I flashed on the very first time I'd met T, when he had used his belt on me and drops of melted wax from a long white candle that tickled and stung my nipples at the same time. I had not been able to think of much else until our next meeting. I also recalled the many times I'd been afraid to see him after that, even as I'd remained fully compelled. I would go, full of dread, the memory of gritting my teeth and breathing like a pregnant woman who's refused an epidural still fresh in my mind from the last time. I'd only had a real hypnotic rush after the first and second meetings—the rest of our dozen or so times together had left me confused and upset, by both his advancing tortures and my reluctance to just say *no*. Whenever I'd tried to talk to him about how I wasn't enjoying the things we were doing as much anymore, he would put his fingers inside me. *Why*, he would ask, *if you don't like it, why is your body so open to me right now? Why are you drenching my hand?* How could I tell what I was in all that?

"Lift up for a second," Phil grunted, pulling a piece of the rope through my legs from the back, positioning the strand so that it ran between my cheeks and in a straight line between my legs.

As soon as I sat down, he pulled the rope taut, making me gasp from both the surprise of it and the sensation. He then held it firmly while threading it through the harness he'd made around my breasts. A minute later, he began tugging rhythmically on the harness in a way that felt like a strong finger pressing between my legs. Grateful to have my attention focused on something besides T, I leaned my head into the back of the chair and closed my eyes, smiling. With his free hand, Phil brushed a strand of hair away from my eyes.

"Do you like this, Marnie?"

His voice was deep, almost gruff, but it came out soft, even a little hesitant. He had been much the same way in the interview—attractive enough to get my attention, but almost shy in his manner toward me, claiming he hoped to learn a lot from me since I was the more experienced player.

"Yes, thank you, sir. My real name's Joan, by the way. Is it okay for you to call me that instead?"

It had been grating on me, the fake sound of that name coming out of his mouth in the middle of something that felt like this. He let the ropes fall slack, and I opened my eyes. He looked almost giddy with delight.

"Nice to meet you, Joan. My name's really Phil."

He tightened the ropes again in his hands, and went back to tugging. A surprisingly short time later, he dropped the ropes for good and began to untie my feet from the chair legs. For all the time it had taken to get me into that position, I was surprised that he would undo his own work so nonchalantly minutes later. I tried not to show any disappointment I felt. The truth was, I could have stayed like that all day, on or off the clock.

"Stand up."

He took my hands in his and raised me up off the chair, then squatted to massage my legs before standing again to work on my arms. I closed my eyes as his muscular fingers applied just the right amount of pressure to skin that still tingled where the ropes had pressed into me.

"When you feel steady enough on your feet, I'd like you to go stand in front of the mirror, a few feet away but facing it, and bend over."

Staring at the slightly fragrant shag carpet in front of my face a few moments later, I asked for permission to put my hands on my knees for balance.

"You may do that if you need to. I'd like you to remain as still as possible otherwise."

"Yes, sir," I murmured, remembering the last time I'd heard the words *remain as still as possible.*

I had been bent over a table in an Orange County hotel room, feet and hands tied to the wooden legs beneath me. It was the third time I'd met with T in person, and when he'd ordered me not to move, I'd taken him to mean *not even your lungs,* as that was nearly the only part of me that had range of motion at that point anyway. I'd begun drawing in slow, shallow breaths to minimize the rise and fall of my chest in the hopes of doing this right; he had already been

THE PLEASURE'S ALL MINE

punishing me for a list of minor mistakes I'd made that day. Using a whip I'd made out of sixteen strands of clothesline that I'd cut, soaked and tied together at his instruction, he'd brought his short but muscular arms up again and again over his head, sometimes brushing the high ceiling with the tips of the homemade whip before bringing it down on my upper back or ass. When I'd cried out too loudly at one point, he'd told me I was to hold still *and* not make a sound. I hadn't known what choice I had then but to breathe deeply and visibly, to take my mind off the urge to scream.

After what had seemed like half an hour to me but could have been a great deal more or less, T had stopped abruptly when he'd noticed an old red stain of something on the table lamp's creamy shade, and had mistakenly taken it to be a drop of my blood, spattered from the whipping. Instead of relief, I'd remained anxious when he let me up, feeling like I'd somehow done something wrong even in how I'd endured his punishment. It had taken a good night's sleep and another twenty-four hours for me to realize that he'd been trying to make me cry, to make noise, all along.

Phil moved in close behind me now and gripped my waist with slightly calloused fingers, holding me gently in front of him as he talked.

"We're going to start slow, and I want you to say 'mercy' if at any point we get into territory that you can't handle. Okay?"

I nodded my head, thinking how much I liked the tone of his voice. It sounded like Phil genuinely had no interest in hurting me in a way that didn't turn me on—as if he would experience it as a mistake on his end, rather than a failure to be masochistic enough on mine. It was different from what I had felt with T. Thinking back, it seemed to me that T's idea of a safe word had been more along the lines of something I could say if I really wanted to interrupt his good time. With Phil, I got the immediate feeling that I, myself, was his good time.

When he began dropping the strands of a leather flogger softly onto my hips, I worried momentarily that he was going to be almost *too* careful with me, that things would never heat up to a noticeable level. At least with T, I'd get an adrenaline rush, if nothing else. Within a few minutes, however, Phil had progressed to a level of intensity that rivaled what I'd experienced with T so many months before.

It was hard for me to believe we were really playing that heavily at first, for how little it took out of me. If anything, I felt like Phil was transferring something *to* me, between the methodical swing of his arm and the pieces of leather that now seemed like a physical extension of his body. Stopping in between sets of twenty strokes, delivered evenly across my upper thighs and ass, he would ask me if I was doing okay, if I was ready to go harder. When he approached me to hear my response, I could feel the warmth of his body emanating from the denim of his jeans as he held himself barely an inch away from me, massaging me in all the places where the flogger had landed. Pushing back into the hands that cupped me, I always answered *yes* and that I was fine, and waited for it to feel like something that was hurting.

"How did you learn to do these things, if you don't have that much experience?" I found myself asking.

Phil was making soft cuffs for my ankles and wrists from several pieces of white rope. He was preparing to attach me to the suspension bar that could be lowered to the floor or lifted toward the ceiling, depending on which way you turned the crank on the wall.

"Oh, I don't know." He laughed sheepishly. "I read a lot of the bondage stuff in books, and I had a few sessions with a pro sub a couple of years ago."

It was only our second session together, but already I felt jealous about the idea of his playing with other people. He had asked me if I could come in to see him this second night in a row, even though I hadn't been on the schedule. I had eagerly admitted to having nothing better to do.

"You have, or haven't, been suspended before?"

"Haven't been," I said, "but I've been curious about it for a while, sir."

He let go of the rope and put his hands on my face, looking at me seriously. I raised my eyebrows back at him, not sure if I was supposed to say something else or just lie there. He smiled and kissed me gently on the forehead.

"I don't think I've ever played with anyone as genuinely sweet as you," he said, picking up the ends of the harness again.

"Oh go on," I joked, waving at him with my half-tied hand. I was embarrassed to think it might show on my face how glad I was to hear it.

He grinned at me again and gave a little shake of his head. "Now let's see if I can get you off the floor without injuring either of us in the process."

As Phil turned the crank on the wall and began lifting me off the floor, I started to swing a little back and forth. I closed my eyes and saw the hilltop park across the street from my childhood home, or rather, the view of Los Angeles below its cliff. The kids in the neighborhood used to go there, even as teenagers, to ride the swings that faced the ledge over the steep, ice plant-covered hill. On a clear day, you could see downtown forty miles away, some of the ocean off to the left, and snow up on Big Bear Mountain if it was that time of year. You could also, if you had that kind of mind, see yourself vaulted out of the swing, either by choice or accident, when it was at its highest point, almost parallel to the upper bar it was attached to. You couldn't see the ground below at that point, only the urban expanse beyond that cliff, as if you were already sailing out into it. *How far could I get, and would it kill me when I landed?* was what I always wondered.

Phil lifted me higher, and suddenly my wrists and ankles began to burn. It was the first time I'd felt anything resembling actual pain with him, and it caused me a mixture of shock and alarm. I couldn't really stand the idea of telling him that we had to stop what we were doing, but I knew the circles of fire on my skin would make me yell soon. I opened my mouth to say something calm and graceful.

"Excuse me, sir."

I tried to clear my throat, realizing for the first time that my head was hanging in such a way that had made it hard to swallow for the last couple of minutes. Instead of helping, the attempted throat clearing made me start to cough, and each small spasm of my body made the ropes on my limbs dig in more deeply and painfully. I panicked.

"It's not—I can't—it's cutting me—please," I started to babble, and then started to cry. Phil let me down as fast as he could and knelt beside me.

"I'm so sorry! What happened? Are you okay?"

He untied me and then held my head in one of his hands, looking at me with concern and fear. I put my hands over my face, ashamed, but unable to stop crying. It wasn't even the pain or the irrational guilt I felt about not being able to take it. Phil's reaction made me think about all the times that T had hurt me in ways I couldn't handle, when I'd begged him to stop, and how he'd never looked at me afterwards the way Phil was looking at me now. I had felt like I loved T. I'd certainly tried to endure the things he wanted to subject me to. And I didn't understand it: Neither his lack of tenderness nor my own willingness to put up with it made any sense to me anymore. It made me feel like I'd helped someone do something really horrible.

Phil took my hands slowly away from my face so that he could rub each of my wrists. "I would never intentionally hurt you. I'm so sorry that happened—"

"No, no," I interrupted him, "it's not that. And I'm okay." I pulled one of my hands up to wipe around my eyes. He kept his soft grip on that same wrist, massaging the whole time.

"So were the ropes too tight, or . . . ?"

"I don't really know what started it. Maybe it was that my weight pulled too much against them? It just started to burn, and then . . ." I shook my head and swiped again at my face. "I think it's just that I really like you, and it reminds me of the last person I really liked."

"I see. And you're not over him." Phil sounded a little disappointed, but understanding.

"It's not even that, really. I've never been with someone who was both really sadistic and really kind, like you. Something about it makes me happy and sad at the same time."

Phil brushed a thumb gently across my cheekbone, wiping it temporarily dry. "So you really like me, huh?" he asked seriously, and when that made me laugh, he laughed too.

I nodded and closed my eyes, and we stayed that way until Hillary's voice cut through on the intercom about ten minutes later. As he helped me up off the floor, he asked if he could see me again the next night.

Phil had not known exactly what time he'd be coming by, so I'd brought a change of clothes with me to my day job and gone right to the dungeon after work. I found Samantha working the desk and no one else around when I got there at six.

The front door buzzed loudly as I was getting dressed, and I took as deep a breath as my new underwire bra would allow before heading toward the lobby.

"I'm here to see Marnie," Phil announced, and held up a hand in greeting when he saw me coming through the kitchen.

"Would you like to talk back here for a minute?"

I motioned behind me toward the Dean Martin, and Phil nodded sweetly at Samantha before following me back. Sometimes I still had trouble believing he was as sexy as he was in session—he had such an exaggerated air of harmlessness about him, otherwise. Even though it wasn't like he came off as a jerk or anything, it still seemed like a bit of a contradiction.

I closed the Dean Martin door behind us, and turned around to a close-up of Phil's button-down shirt. He put his arms around me, and I turned my cheek against his chest, resting my hands in the small of his back. I could hear the whisper of his lungs filling up and emptying through the thin cotton covering his chest.

"I didn't really need to talk with you first, I just wanted to hug you before anything else." He sounded sheepish.

"That's not very sadistic of you," I teased, and he laughed and hugged me harder. "No, it's cute," I said seriously, and he let me go so we could talk face-to-face.

"Is that very impressive to a submissive—for a dominant to be 'cute'?" He was smiling when he asked, but didn't seem to be joking.

"I don't know what anyone else wants," I shrugged, "but I find everything about you impressive."

He leaned forward and kissed my forehead. "My kind of gal—low standards!" he laughed.

"That's not true," I shook my head. "It's just—I don't know if you can understand what it's like for me, what a relief you are for me. I've never met anyone who I could play this intensely with who didn't also get on my nerves somehow." He chuckled at that but I went on. "Really. You lack a sort of, I don't know, arrogance that I really had begun to think was part of the genetic makeup of dominant men." At that he laughed out loud.

"Lacking a sort of arrogance—I've never had a compliment like that before."

"I probably sound pretty judgemental, huh?" Now I felt sheepish.

He put his hands on my shoulders. "You sound like someone who's careful about who she plays with. As well you should be. You're quite special."

"Thank you." I pulled him close to me in another hug and then stepped back. "We should probably get back out there, or they'll start to worry."

Phil paid Samantha for two hours while I got our usual supply of toys from the little closet. We didn't end up using any of them this time; neither of us seemed to be able to get enough of him just using his hands on me. Within a few minutes of our arrival upstairs, he had me bent over with my elbows on the bench to hold me up while he massaged my lower back gently and then ran his hands over as much of the rest of me as he could reach. I could feel how careful he was with his own body, bringing it close enough behind me that I kept getting a slight tickle from the fabric of his pants against the backs of my thighs, but still holding it firmly apart from me as well. When he put his hand briefly between my legs and moved two fingers in a circular motion over the most sensitive part, I didn't stop him, the way I had with the other couple of clients who'd tried it.

"Can I tell you something, sir?"

He pulled his hand away and moved beside me, leaning down to hear.

I felt a little awkward, then. I had meant to try and say something about how he could touch me under my G-string if he wanted to, but once his hand was gone from that area, it felt like a pushy request. Then I felt anxious as well. What if he didn't want to touch me there, like that? What if he thought, because of my job, that I was someone who might not be clean enough down there to put a bare hand on? I wished I hadn't opened my mouth, convinced now that it was a disastrous choice, but he was looking at me so intently and with such openness, I felt like it would be an insult to turn away from him.

"I just was gonna say," I cleared my throat, "I could take this off if you want me to." I straightened my arms and took one hand off the bench, pulling at the waistband of my G-string. "But we don't have to," I said in a rush, before he could answer.

I swear it almost looked like he blushed in the faint light of the room. "Thank you for offering. But I don't want to do anything you're not honestly comfortable with."

"I wouldn't have brought it up if I were uncomfortable." I looked into his face, no longer worried about what he would think of me, of my body. "I want you to feel like you can touch me everywhere." I turned to stare again at the bench in front of me. "I want to feel what it's like to be touched inside. By you." I held my breath, afraid that this last might have been over the line.

He moved behind me again, and I sighed with relief when his fingers hooked the elastic around my waist and pulled it down over my hips. He helped me step out of my underwear and then placed it neatly on the bench in front of me.

His finger felt much softer inside me than it sometimes did

against my skin, the familiar roughness melting away so that there was only warmth and an easy pressure. I had a few seconds of worrying about what I was doing. What if these rooms were secretly rigged with hidden cameras, or Hillary found out in some other way? Would she or the others understand what it was like for me? Had it ever been like this for any of them? Or was I the only one who ever felt tempted, let alone gave into it?

When our time was up, Phil helped me collect the things we hadn't used and then took me by the shoulders as we were about to go back down the stairs.

"I'd love to just talk with you, if you'd be comfortable with that. If it's not too late for you after the shift is over, I'd love to buy you a cup of coffee."

I couldn't think of what to say at first. I was thrilled that he wanted to see me outside of here; I knew also that it was even more against the rules than the naked touching I'd initiated earlier. *It's not fair, though. Am I really supposed to pass up the chance to like someone this much, just because we accidentally met here instead of somewhere else?*

"I would love that."

He leaned his face in toward me, and I had enough time to stop him if I'd wanted to, but instead I leaned a little toward him and kissed him back when his lips brushed against mine.

"But we have to be quiet about it," I said, pushing him slightly away. "I could get in trouble if they knew I was going to meet you after work."

"I won't say a word."

We agreed that he would wait for me outside in his car and follow me wherever I wanted to go after that. I took him to the Bob's Big Boy a few blocks from my apartment building. I had to get up early to go to the office the next morning and didn't want to have to drive a long way home later.

"I've never felt like this with anyone before. I'm a little in shock from it, frankly," Phil said.

"It's the same for me," I agreed, and we both fell stiffly silent as the waitress leaned in with his cup of coffee and my lemonade.

"Really? So with the other dom that you'd told me about, the one from your personal life—surely you've had some feeling like this before?"

It was a sincere question, not some attempt to get me to reassure him that he was better. I shook my head, and glanced at the people in the booth across from us. I could see their mouths moving but couldn't make out what they were saying, and decided the opposite was probably true as well.

"I felt . . . excited by him, but I never felt this happy." I looked over at Phil. He was frowning, concerned. "I never trusted him, I guess is what it was. Not like I trust you."

He reached a hand across the slightly sticky tabletop, his fingers in an open search for my hand. I reached my own hand across and let him hold me.

"There's something I wanted to talk to you about." He looked serious, but there was something hesitant in his tone as well.

I knew that I felt attracted to him beyond what I'd felt for any other clients. But if we started some kind of personal relationship, would he at some point ask me to quit the dungeon job? And would that be a fair request? I'd known since my first shift that I wanted to be able to quit my straight day job as soon as possible; would I be able to stomach it again indefinitely just for Phil? Did I even *want* to have to make that kind of a trade-off just for a relationship? Although we hadn't talked about what he did for a living, I had the impression that he wasn't exactly a rich guy who'd be offering to support me. He'd made some remark during our second session about how after the next time, which was tonight, it might be a while before he could see me again. I figured his disposable income had run out for the month, and was flattered that he'd felt compelled to spend it all on seeing me so many times in a row. *If all else fails, just try to look thoughtful for a minute or so, until you can figure out what you want to say.*

"I know I told you I couldn't see you for a little while after tonight. God, I don't want to hurt you—"

"It's okay . . . what?"

I thought he meant to reassure me that it wasn't anything personal, the fact that he wouldn't be able to afford to see me for a little while. I was just about to say that I didn't care, that we didn't have to see each other at the dungeon anymore, that I wanted to take things slow but that I didn't want to have to wait to be in his hands again until he had more money in them, when he blurted out his own declaration of love.

"I adore my wife, she's the most understanding, loving, supportive person in the world; she's my whole life. We've been on vacation here this week, and she has no idea that I'm into this stuff. I'm sorry, Joan. I couldn't have imagined having these feelings for anyone but my wife, before I met you. It's so confusing. But I can't leave her. We're going back home to Canada tomorrow."

I didn't have to fake a thoughtful silence, as it turned out. I could not for the life of me think of what to say. Somewhere in the back of my mind, I'd realized that someone as cute and decent as he was would have been able to get married by his age if he'd ever wanted to. And I certainly knew that many men came to places like the Dominion *because* they were married, not in spite of it. They were with women they loved, but like me, had needs they hadn't been able to fulfill any place else. Still, I'd certainly hoped. I'd hoped that the way Phil looked at me meant something as sweet and open as it felt, not something that would make another woman cry if she found out about it.

"I thought you might be. Married, I mean. I guess I didn't ask earlier because it would've killed it for me," I finally managed to say quietly.

"I understand," he nodded, lowering his eyes. "I don't blame you. I don't like me very much for it either."

"No, I mean it would've had that effect early on, but now it's kind of too late. In every way, I guess," I said, and laughed dryly.

I already felt how I felt. And it didn't matter. He was leaving tomorrow, married or not. *I am not going to start crying in Bob's Big Boy.*

As we waited for the check, I tried to tell myself that it wasn't a bad thing—that objectively speaking, it was, in fact, wonderful that

I'd been able to feel this way at all. And that, in all likelihood, we had nothing in common outside of the dungeon anyway, which might have been a more disheartening discovery than his marriage and Canadian citizenship, if we'd had the chance to date. *We barely know each other. I'm not in love with him. Nothing is different about my life than it was before I met him a few days ago, and I wasn't crying then.*

I checked the rearview mirror three times after I pulled into the street, watching him turn north, back toward the hotel where his wife was waiting. It was only when I saw my face in the bathroom mirror a few minutes later that the knot in my stomach untied itself, shaking loose in great heaving sobs.

# SIX

"**I KNOW YOU** know this, but I have to say it anyway. You should never have met him outside of here alone."

*I shouldn't have met him, period,* I thought to myself. *The whole thing's ruined for me now.*

"It's a safety thing, Marnie," Hillary continued. "I'm not mad at you about it."

No one else had come in yet for the afternoon shift, so we had the reception area to ourselves.

"It's not that," I shook my head miserably.

I'd e-mailed her about Phil a couple of days earlier in a semi-panic. I'd thought I was a pretty resilient person, but I had only felt worse since the last night I'd seen Phil. My note had been more of a plea for help than a confession. *How do I get it to go back to the way it was before, when I hadn't known what I was missing?*

Hillary sighed loudly, but spoke gently. "You just—you can't really let your heart get too involved here."

"I know, and I don't normally feel like this with clients, even when it's really fun. I don't know what happened."

Hillary was quiet for a few seconds. "You're gonna feel that way about other people, Marnie." She sounded like she was just realizing what my problem was. "You know that, right?"

I looked at the desk between us and shrugged. I'd been searching on and off for so long. How could something this random and unusual happen again any time soon?

Hillary laughed softly. "You have to believe me. I did this for *years.* He's just the first client you've felt this way about. He's not the last, and he's not *the one,* okay?"

I said nothing, just listened.

"The trick is to be able to keep a hold of yourself even when it's great," she went on. "Hell, especially when it's great. You don't know it now, but, in a way, you're lucky that guy left. Otherwise, you might've ended up seeing him for free."

Hillary's warning surprised me. How could she have known that I'd been about to tell Phil I'd happily be his nonprofessional submissive right before he'd dropped the Canadian husband bomb? What if he hadn't dropped it? Did I have to forfeit a personal life if I wanted to keep doing this professionally?

"If two people end up liking each other in a serious way, are they never supposed to see each other without money being involved?"

"Marnie, Marnie, Marnie," she sighed. "Yes. Sometimes people who meet in session do end up falling for each other, and it becomes a more personal relationship. Between you and me, that's how I met my own master."

Hillary had told me that she was still submissive in her personal life, back when I'd interviewed for the job, but I was surprised to hear that she'd met her current boyfriend through work so long ago.

"But he had seen me for *years* in session. He was more protective about my taking his money than I was. You gotta understand—lots of guys out there aren't the same way. They see you getting attached, they'll use it to their advantage. This is our *livelihood.* You wouldn't ask him to stop accepting his paycheck just because he likes *you,* would you?"

I thought about what she said. I had definitely worried at times that it meant something insincere or sleazy about me that I liked making money this way. Hillary made it sound like a matter of self-care, not greed.

"Vanessa will watch out for you today, won't you?" she called out, as Vanessa came through the front door with her session clothes in one hand and cup of coffee in the other.

"What's the matter, Marnie, dear?" She sounded half asleep.

"Nothing, I'm fine." I waved a hand at her. "Thanks for talking to me, Hillary. I feel better."

"Good." Hillary pushed her stool back from the table. "I gotta get going, I just came by to do the books."

And I did feel better, really. Hillary had made me feel like my fresh heartache over Phil was almost an ancient tradition, like a kinky rookie's rite of passage into a more grounded, and exciting, relationship with this job. It sparked visions of a future self, happily absorbed in a pleasurable web of safely-defined connections with clients, and the growing bank account to go with it.

When the phone rang a short while later, Vanessa's heels clicked loudly through the back hall and kitchen as she ran up to answer it.

"A man's coming in to spank you in half an hour," she told me cheerfully after hanging up.

*Good,* I thought. *And no matter how much fun he is, I'm going to keep a hold of myself, just like Hillary said.*

"It's not you, I'm sorry sir, I just . . . I'm sad about something else right now, I'm sorry."

I had started weeping quietly about twenty minutes into our half-hour session. The British client named Tom looked worried. He'd been using a leather paddle on me, not hard at all, as we had acted out his fantasy of stern-professor-punishes-tardy-college-student.

"No, no, it's not a problem for me," he said. "I'm just concerned about *you.*"

I tried to think of how to explain it without going into detail. Before I'd met Phil, this would have been a dream session for me. We were doing stuff I liked to do; it was easy on my body because he wasn't into causing real pain; and the man himself had that cute, freckly, English type of face that collapsed into pure sweetness when he smiled—which he'd done during our interview when I'd told him that it would be my first real role-playing session. I didn't count the few minutes of pretending that I'd done with Bill on my first day.

"Why don't you have a seat, then, and we'll talk for a minute."

He motioned to the leopard-print bench, the same one I'd been on with Phil a couple of nights before. *It just doesn't feel right to be in here with someone else.*

"I like you, and I think this is really fun," I wept. It was finally too ridiculous for me then, and I started to laugh. I caught the nervous look on his face and shook my head. "Sorry, this is just kind of weird for me."

"Not at all," he patted my shoulder. "It's okay with me if you want to continue, and it's okay with me if you don't."

I wanted to tell him the truth—that I wished he could just come back another day. I knew this ache I was feeling would pass. I knew now that it was simply something Phil had made me more aware of—my craving to feel controlled and cared about at the same time—not something that was specific to Phil, and Phil alone. But I was afraid to tell Tom any of it. I worried he would think I was desperate to find a replacement for Phil and that I might glom onto him like a drowning person. Never mind that his fantasy hadn't included playing the role of a therapist.

Suddenly our time was up, saving me from both an explanation and a decision. Still, I felt horrible, like I had ripped him off somehow, cheated him of those last few minutes of fantasy fulfillment that might have put a spring in his step for the rest of the week, for all I knew. Since the money he'd plunked down wasn't all mine, I didn't feel like I had the authority to offer part of it back to him. With his polite British murmuring and handshaking on the way out, it was hard for me to tell whether he was disappointed or merely perplexed. Worried now that I was bad for business, I tried to talk to Vanessa about it. When I couldn't get a word out before breaking down, she jumped up from her chair at the desk and grabbed my shoulders.

"What happened, Marnie? *Samantha, stop that man!*" she yelled into the television room.

I heard the pages of a magazine flapping together as Samantha, who must have come in while I was upstairs, darted out from the television room to find out what was going on.

"No, no!" I said quickly, "it's not him, he was great." *That's all he needs. First his session devolves into a nervous breakdown scenario— not a common fetish—and then he gets jumped by two angry dommes on his way out.*

"What's the matter, then?" Vanessa looked concerned.

It all came spilling out of me: what had happened with Phil; how I'd thought it would take my mind off him to come in and work today; how playing with Tom had only made it unexpectedly worse. What chance did I have of succeeding in this business if I couldn't master the most basic principle of sex work—faking it? Vanessa and Samantha listened with worried faces until I finished, and then erupted in a flurry of attempted solutions.

"Come sit down over here," Vanessa commanded briskly, and pulled me to one of the softer chairs in the lobby. "We'll get you something to drink."

She dashed into the other room and came back with a small cotton blanket. As she bundled me up, Samantha came striding toward me with a hot cup of black coffee from the kitchen.

"Oh, thank you," I said, embarrassed. "I'm sorry. I don't want to be rude, but I don't drink coffee."

"That's okay, honey!" Samantha said quickly, as if she feared it might set me off again. She put the cup down on the front desk and came back to hover near Vanessa, who was still fussing slightly with the blanket.

"There!" Vanessa said uncertainly, as if she hoped, but didn't quite believe, that it would hold me together.

I half entertained the idea of pretending I wasn't warm enough, just to get her to spend another couple of minutes smoothing soft fabric around my shoulders and tucking corners underneath me. I'd never seen two people act so tenderly in the middle of such social discomfort, and the unexpected sweetness of it got me choked up all over again. I'd had no idea how badly I wanted people just to be nice to me. The realization of it—first with Phil, and then Samantha and Vanessa—tore me open in ways that felt simultaneously wonderful and excruciating.

"Oh God, she's inconsolable!" Vanessa yelped. She turned to Samantha, eyes wide and pleading. "*Help her!*"

I started to try and reassure them that what I was feeling wasn't exactly bad, but before I could get a word out, Samantha grabbed my head and pulled my face into her substantial bosom.

"It's okay, it's okay," she purred awkwardly, holding my head with one hand and stroking the back of my hair with the other. Although I couldn't stand the feel of anything touching my face, even anything as beautiful as Samantha's chest, it would have felt selfish, somehow, to pull myself away. They were trying so hard to make me feel better, these two leather-clad women whose primary business was clamps, paddles, and humiliation scenes. My urge to comfort them for their failure to comfort me calmed me down, and, after another minute of quietly inhaling Samantha's cleavage, I was released and allowed to sit back in my chair without further molestation.

"Why don't you just go home for the day, sweetheart? I'll let Hillary know. And," Vanessa walked quickly into the kitchen to check the schedule, "another sub is coming on shift in half an hour. We'll be fine."

Samantha pulled me up and steered me into the television room, where I quickly stripped off my work dress and stockings and pulled on the T-shirt and jeans that she handed me from my bag. The two of them hugged me briefly and hurried me out the door as if scared that I might change my mind, and I could only imagine that they were as relieved as I was once I was out in the harsh and distracting daylight of that Saturday afternoon.

After crying my way through the rest of the weekend, I woke up Monday morning with a head that felt remarkably washed clean. As relieved as I was to be mostly over the sorrow of the previous week, I was even more relieved by the thought that popped into my head during my lunch hour. *If you're there more often, you'll surely meet more men, more quickly, who will feel as good as Phil did.* It was a brilliant plan, I realized. Of *course* I should start working at the dungeon full time! I used the computer at work to e-mail Hillary and ask for more shifts, and used the last fifteen minutes of my workday to give the boss my two weeks' notice.

"I've gotten an offer to help my friend with scripts and editing at her new production company," I lied, hoping it sounded like an offer I couldn't refuse rather than a rejection of the unspoken boredom I felt in my current position.

"We'll miss you, but I'm sure you'll be great at your new job."

Even knowing they didn't really need me, it stung a little to have to leave such nice people behind. *They deserve someone who's happier to be here,* I consoled myself, and stopped on the way home that night to buy myself a couple of new outfits to celebrate my move.

As I entered the lounge area for my first ex-secretary shift, I could see from where the new sub sat that her legs were about twice as long as mine, darkly tanned and sculpted like a dancer's. When she stood to introduce herself, my worst fears were confirmed. The rest of her body, previously folded up ambiguously in the easy chair, was as long and lean as her legs. To top it all off, her face was not only cute, but conveyed something almost sublimely sweet and vulnerable. I would not even have the consolation prize of being able to dislike her on a rational level.

"My name's Ryan. You must be Marnie."

"Nice to meet you," I said, feeling the warmth of her delicately long fingers in mine. I was overcome by a sudden feeling of noticeable bloat by comparison.

"That's such a cute top. It's funny, I have a pair of shorts that match it exactly. I made them myself." Ryan had the tiniest lisp when she spoke, and I wondered resentfully if there was anything about her that wasn't adorable.

"Wow, you make clothes? That's neat." I smiled politely, determined not to let my reflexive hostility toward this threatening creature show through.

Ryan shrugged modestly. "Just little costumes and stuff. I used to be a dancer. It was cheaper to make my own outfits," she laughed. That explained the perfect body. "Hey, I bet they'd fit you. I'll bring 'em in for you next time we work together. When are you on again?"

"Really? Um . . . wow. Thanks." I didn't know if I was supposed to offer her something else then in return—money, or something of mine? I'd never met anyone who'd just offered me a present—and one that was kind of perfect for me, if it really would match my purple, velvety bra top—within the first two minutes of shaking hands. What the hell kind of girl was this?

Over the next five hours, I found out. She was the kind of girl that every man who walked through the door wanted to pay good money to tie up, tickle, tease, and otherwise pleasurably torment for hours straight. She was the kind of girl that I could not ever hope to get chosen over; the kind who, really through no fault of her own, rendered me perfectly invisible. When I'd looked at the schedule for the next two weeks, this Ryan person was working every single shift that I was. I saw a clock in my mind, hour and minute hands whirling crazily, and the word *loser* pulsing constantly on top of it in bright neon lettering.

Ryan's abrupt and overshadowing presence in my fantasyland felt grossly unfair. She had a boyfriend. She was good at stripping, and could get all the attention any one person should need from that job alone. What malevolent force in the cosmos had sent her to my neck of the woods, to start hijacking *my* good time? It had to be a mistake. Seated miserably in the lounge for the next eight shifts straight, I began to wonder if my enthusiastic transition to full-time kink hadn't been the real mistake.

Noticing my ever-present, unhappy face in the lounge during this period, Vanessa suggested I try a little extracurricular advertising in an effort to liven up my shifts. It seemed my Internet account came with the ability to set up a free home page, and several of the women at the Dominion already had their own. Thinking things couldn't get any worse, I put up one of my photos from the Dominion Web site, along with a description of the kinds of things I would and wouldn't do in session. Within hours, I'd received over a dozen new messages in my in-box. It turned out most of them were from men who either wanted sex to be part of the session or to "woo" me into playing with them on a personal level for free. But I could hardly believe my luck when I opened the following two messages.

*Dear Marnie . . . You look great and you sound like genuine fun—rare thing to find in a pro sub. Wondering if you would consider ever sessioning outside the Dominion? I'm afraid the possible interaction with other men in the front lobby puts me off.*

*Dear submissive Marnie . . . . I'd love a session with you, and want to know whether you allow yourself to get fully naked, and whether you would submit to a scenario where I make you urinate in a bowl while I watch.*

The idea of finding a way to see these clients outside the Dominion immediately excited me. I would actually get to play with someone again, instead of watching the doe-eyed Ryan get all the action. I knew that as "independent contractors" at the Dominion, employees were not allowed to work privately at the same time. Still, I thought there must be some way for me to meet with clients on my own that would make Hillary happy as well. I needed the money, and if I could find a place to see them that was safe enough but offered more privacy, I bet that I could charge a little more than the hourly rate at the Dominion. If I split it fifty-fifty with Hillary, how could she object? It made sense to me, and I could hardly wait for my next shift so I could break the good news.

· · ·

"I can't allow that," Hillary shook her head stiffly.

"Oh," I said, too surprised to think of anything else to say at first. I had found her eating lunch in the kitchen after changing for my shift that next Saturday. "Is it a matter of . . . I mean are you concerned about—Why isn't it allowed?"

"I've invested way too much money here to allow someone to take business away. I spend hundreds a month—thousands a *year*—on advertising in as many places as I can find so that clients can find us, not to mention all the work and money I put into keeping the physical space up and running."

"But that's not what I'm talking about," I interrupted quickly. "I'm not talking about seeing clients that I meet *here*. I'm talking about the kinds of guys who wouldn't be coming in here to spend their money in the first place. I don't understand why that would be anything but good for you, if I'm giving you a cut."

"I have no way of knowing who you'd be seeing outside and who you wouldn't. Besides, no respectable dominant client would try to get you to see him outside the protective environment of a place like this. Anyone who's seriously in the scene knows that subs need the safety of a chaperone. The only reason a guy would try to see you without one is if he wants to do things to you that he knows a chaperone would bust him for."

*Bust* him for? Like the way the protective arms of the Dominion had "busted" Daniel the Torture-Tickler on my second shift? I understood that the business of letting strangers dominate me in various ways was a risky one. But I didn't need a custodial parent any more than the dommes did. Nor was I interested in exclusively courting the kinds of clients who saw women like me in those childlike terms.

"I guess it's just hard for me to understand—"

"That's because you're a lot less experienced in the scene, Marnie. You practically just started here, and you've said you only had one S/M relationship in your personal life. I've been doing this in my personal life and as a business for the last twenty years. I know what I'm talking about."

She had a point about being more experienced than me, but it didn't ease my aggravation. I knew I could make money outside the Dominion, I knew I would be honorable about it, and my gut told me that Hillary was all wrong about the kinds of people who would see me on my own. It seemed useless to talk to her about it anymore, though. I told her I understood what she was saying, and would not do sessions both inside and outside of the Dominion at the same time. And while I hadn't given up on my hope for outside sessions, I meant what I told her. I left out the part about how I'd be looking into the possibility of going independent like some of the dommes I'd heard about before.

Once it settled in that I was really planning to leave, I realized that I didn't have the foggiest idea of how to go about it. What would be the etiquette for quitting a place like the Dominion? Was I supposed to give two weeks' notice like at a real job, write a letter of resignation, or wave good-bye and take to my heels whenever I felt like it? I didn't feel like I could ask any of the other women without the risk of it getting back to Hillary before I did.

"Marnie, you have a twelve o'clock with a man named Stanley. He's a regular, pretty nice guy, mostly into bondage and light corporal stuff."

Hillary was at the front desk that morning, and told me about the session as soon as I walked in the door. Neither her expression nor her tone of voice indicated any residual tension from our talk a few days before. I felt a sudden pang of guilt knowing that I'd be wrecking our truce sometime in the very near future. However, I quashed it with the reminder that she hadn't left me much choice. I thanked her and headed to the back to get dressed. A beautiful brunette with gorgeous olive skin was already there changing.

"Hi, I'm Angela," she smiled.

"I'm Marnie," I smiled back. After a couple of moments of awkward silence, I spoke again. "Is this your first shift?"

"I started last night. I'm still kind of scared, though," she laughed abruptly and looked away.

I had already pegged her for a sub, what with the cream-colored collar she'd fastened around her neck, and debated whether to try and console her or compound her worries. I didn't have any bad feelings toward her personally, but this had been my first scheduled session without Ryan working at the same time. Now I had a younger version of Salma Hayek to contend with? *This is going to suck.* And yet, even with my rising insecurity, I couldn't really stand the thought of treating her badly or seeing her upset. *Fuck it. I'm almost out of here anyway.*

"Are you just scared because it's a new thing, or are you actually afraid of getting hurt here?"

"Both, I guess."

"I was pretty nervous when I started, too," I offered. "I don't know many of the other subs here, but the dommes I know have all been really cool. Talking to them relaxed me a lot when I first got here. And if there's anything in particular that you're worried about, you can always ask me, if that helps."

"Thanks, Marnie."

I couldn't tell if she felt any better yet, but I certainly did. I wasn't necessarily happy about helping my competition feel better— I came here to feel sexy, not like some kind of kinky den mother—but I knew I would have been even unhappier if I'd felt guilty about being mean to her.

"No problem," I sighed. "And just so you know, I've mostly had a really great time here, so far. I wouldn't be here if there were bad things happening in session all the time."

Angela nodded and seemed about to say something else, but Hillary's voice came over the intercom, cutting her off.

"Marnie, Stanley is here to see you."

"Thanks," I said toward the small white box on the wall. I turned back to Angela. "You'll do great."

A short, slight man with graying hair and a lightly stained work shirt was shifting his feet in the reception area when I got there. I introduced myself and was about to ask Hillary where we should do the interview when I heard footsteps behind me.

"Oh good," I said to Stanley, "Angela's coming out here, so we can talk back there."

We passed her and Stanley almost bumped into me as his feet kept moving while his eyes stayed on my shift mate. He gave me a reluctant and obviously forced smile, thought better of it and turned to Hillary.

"Is she available right now?" he nodded toward the television room.

"Uh, well, yes she is . . ."

"Will your feelings be hurt if I session with her instead?" he turned back to me.

I felt like someone had knocked the air out of me, and I looked at Hillary without answering. It wasn't the idea of missing a chance to be alone with this somewhat squirrelly guy, or even the loss of potential income that bothered me by this point. It was just so beyond humiliating, to be looked in the face and told, in front of a witness, no less, that someone better had just come along.

"Here, here's twenty dollars so your feelings won't be hurt, okay?"

Stanley ended the impasse by pulling a wrinkled bill out of his pocket and holding it out to me. I looked at his hand, looked at Hillary, looked back at his hand. My pride wanted me to take the money and rip it in half right in his face, to tell him sarcastically that my hurt feelings were selling for considerably more these days. But then I thought, *the way things have been going, this may be the last twenty dollars you see for a while, lady.* I knew then that it was time to go. I grabbed the bill without saying a word and stalked into the television room, yanking the curtain closed behind me. Taylor sat in one of the overstuffed chairs, reading a magazine as usual. Angela was sitting near the TV set, her hands clasped tightly in her lap, attempting a casual look on her face as she scanned the furniture and walls of the room.

"He wants to session with you instead, Angela," I said. "And I'm done. I quit."

"*What?* Marnie, no! What's going on?" Taylor dropped her magazine.

"Bullshit. That's what's going on." I saw the look of horror on Angela's face and felt even worse. "Hey, it's not your fault. You didn't do anything wrong. You're just very cute; that's nothing you've done on purpose. I've been thinking about leaving, anyway. It's not your fault that guy's a dick. I'm upset with him, not you," I finished, and went to the closet to grab my stuff.

"Don't leave like this! I'll go talk to Hillary," Taylor insisted, coming over to me.

"Thanks, Taylor, but please don't. I really liked hanging out with you between sessions, but I can't stay here. I'm not making any money, and now I'm doing free five-minute humiliation scenes! Wait—my mistake. I did get paid twenty dollars." I scowled and shook my head.

"Angela, could you come out here, please?" Hillary's voice cut into the room.

I waited until I heard Angela walk Stanley into the back before going out to tell Hillary I was leaving. I wasn't sure what to say. I felt badly that Hillary had said nothing to Stanley about treating me like that, but then I knew she wasn't in the business of teaching men to act right. She was in the business of getting their money in exchange for sessions with her "independent contractors." But what kind of independence was this? Could I really have expected her to try and shame him into seeing me instead—a session neither of us would have enjoyed at that point—or risk losing his business altogether?

"I'm sorry, I can't work here anymore," was what I finally managed. I held my breath.

"Okay."

Hillary didn't look up from the ledger she was writing in. At first I thought she must be mad at me, but then I realized it was probably just resignation. Maybe, since our talk about outside sessions, she had been expecting me to leave at any second anyway. It made me sad that I wasn't leaving on better terms. I had felt so happy here, such a short time ago. But since I had, in fact, been planning to leave, maybe this was as good a way as any.

As soon as I got home, I went online to look up the only name I could remember from Vanessa's lecture and the ads in *Whips and*

*Chains.* I found Mistress Catherine's phone number on her Web site and called to find out if she would rent her space to me by the hour for my two potential sessions. When she offered to do whatever I needed to make me safe there as well, some of what I had just felt at the Dominion started washing away. It still felt as if something solid had given way underneath me, but for the moment, listening to this stranger assure me that with the right ambition and advertising I could soon have my own bustling pro sub business, I still felt cheerful. Maybe I had made a grave mistake, and maybe this was the universe's way of telling me to go back where I belonged. But maybe not. A few days later I'd booked my first appointment at Catherine's. The client, the one who had e-mailed to ask me about peeing in a bowl, had agreed to my asking price of two hundred and fifty dollars per hour, fifty of which would go to Catherine. I had agreed to bring my own bowl.

If I'd known their last names and home addresses, I would have sent Hillary and Stanley thank you cards.

# SEVEN

**"BACK HERE, MARNIE!"** Catherine's voice came from the far end of a long, wide hallway.

I'd been buzzed into a large brick warehouse somewhere near the garment district of downtown Los Angeles. The neighborhood was deserted, even though it was only around seven thirty. Inside Catherine's front door was a steep set of hardwood stairs, at the top of which I found a huge open space that made up the front part of the loft. The "dungeon" rooms were in the back half—three large areas separated by thin plaster walls and heavy wooden doors.

I had heard muffled conversation as I entered, and wondered who else was here. Maybe another mistress had a session scheduled around the same time as mine? When I got to where Catherine was, I was surprised to see her stretched out, face down, on a massage table. She appeared to be nude, covered from just below her shoulders to mid-calf with a thick terry cloth towel. Her head was turned toward a small, half-naked man at her feet.

"That was good, Bob. You can go clean the bathroom now, and then draw me a hot bath when you're done."

The man nodded silently and snapped the lid closed on a bottle of massage oil, setting it on a shelf next to various sizes of clamps, cuffs, and small paddles that were arranged like so many knickknacks against the wall nearest the door. His eyes never left the ground, and Catherine did not introduce us before he hurried out of the room to complete his chores. I watched him go, his blue boxer shorts rustling between his short legs as he passed me on his way into the hall.

"Hey," Catherine's voice was low and relaxed.

"Hi," I smiled.

The parts of her skin that I could see were shiny with oil from the massage. There was something about the scene I'd walked in on that felt even more exotic than any overtly kinky exchange I might have otherwise witnessed. A session where a servile man pampered her and did her household chores, without any stern tone of voice or pain involved? It was a different view of male submission than any I'd seen so far.

"I put a space heater in the room in case you get cold," Catherine said, sitting up and letting the towel fall from her torso.

Her dark blonde hair fell in waves down her back and across her shoulders, both revealing and covering her small white breasts as she hopped off the table and exposed the rest of her long, slender body. She had even creamy skin, wide red mouth, and black-lined eyes.

"Thank you," I said, feigning an interest in some of the floggers I'd spotted hanging behind the door.

I wondered if I was the only woman who felt like a happy peeping Tom every time another woman decided *it's just us girls* and casually bared all in front of me. It wasn't as if I felt the urge to go fondle myself in the bushes after seeing live naked women, but that I wondered if it made me more of some *other* kind of pervert for liking it so much, the way that I thought an innocent but horny sixteen-year-old boy might.

Catherine retrieved a short silk robe from a hook on the wall and tied its sash around her small waist.

"Do you want me to check in on you once you guys start?"

I snapped out of my reverie and gave her question some thought. I did like the idea of more, rather than less, safety now that I was on my own. Having Catherine close by would actually be more reassuring than anything I'd felt at the Dominion. At the same time, I knew that if I were to succeed as a pro sub on my own, I would need to present myself, as much as was reasonably possible, as being entirely available to each man who wanted to session with me. If I gave any impression of "belonging" to a mistress who was watching out for me, it could interfere with the fantasy I knew these men were looking to fulfill.

"Would there be a way for you to look in on us without it being very obvious?"

"Yeah, that's what the curtains are for. See?" She walked past me to the open door and pushed it closed. There was a large round window in the middle of it, covered by a velvety material hanging on a dull metal rod. "Every door has a window in it. Just pull the curtain open before your session, and if he says anything, tell him it's the house rules for all your new clients; nothing you can do about it. I'll walk by once or twice during your session to have a peek, and he'll never know I'm there."

It sounded great, but then I realized she'd be seeing what *I* was doing as well. We hadn't talked yet about any rules she might have for people who rented from her. I guessed they might not be as restrictive as the rules at the Dominion, but I didn't want to find out in an awkward way that I had crossed some line.

"I feel like I should tell you that I plan to be totally naked in my sessions if my clients ask for that. If that creates any weird kind of legal liability for you and you're not okay with it—"

Catherine cut me off with a short laugh. "I don't care about that, Marnie. Don't all subs get naked?"

"I don't know," I answered honestly. "We weren't allowed to take off our G-strings at the Dominion, so I figured it was against the law everywhere . . ." I trailed off uncertainly.

"From what I've heard, all the subs there are doing it, anyway."

I looked at her in genuine shock. "Really?"

"You seriously didn't know?"

"They told me it was against the rules!" I said, feeling slightly defensive.

"Welcome to the real world," Catherine snickered. "Anyway, I don't care *what* you do in your sessions, as long as you're happy doing it."

"Okay." It sounded so heavenly already—my own rules, no competition swishing by to bum me out, and a person whose sole concern was to keep an eye out for me. I did miss the comforting busyness of the Dominion a little, but every day I'd been away from there had brought back a little more of my confidence. I was falling fast for Catherine and her private dungeon space.

"This is the room you'll be using," Catherine walked past me and I followed her across the hall.

I looked around the cavernous room and felt that familiar mixture of nervousness and excitement that I still got in graphically kinky settings. The huge, low bondage table in the middle looked like a water bed to me, with its slightly puffy black leather mattress and the thick wooden frame surrounding it. *We could do a whole session on that little island alone,* I thought, even after noticing the large iron "bird cage" and old fashioned wooden stocks at the far end. Every wall was a cluster of implements hanging on sturdy black hooks—floggers, leather wrist and ankle cuffs, long whips, wooden and leather and even Lucite paddles. There were also latex hoods that looked like faces sucked empty and moaning with vacant eye and mouth holes. The hoods creeped me out. I would never be able to wear them, even if I wasn't so uptight about having things touch my face. Anyway, I didn't want to play with anyone who needed not to see me while they did things to me.

"We aren't clock-watchers around here, so I'll just knock after it's been more than an hour if I don't see you," Catherine said.

A loud *ding-dong* bounced through the loft.

"That must be Marcus," I said, announcing the name of the client who'd made an eight o'clock appointment with me.

"I'll be in here if you need me." Catherine motioned toward the room where Bob had been massaging her. "Have fun."

Marcus had wanted me to be completely nude for our session, so I hadn't needed to change into anything before he got there. I swung open the front door and stood nervously in my jeans and T-shirt.

"You must be Marnie."

Marcus smiled at me without moving for a few seconds. He was striking. He looked to be in his late forties, with dark brown eyes, cherry red lips, and white hair that fell in soft waves to his earlobes. He was about a foot taller than me, on the lean side, and the skin of his palms and fingers was soft and cool from the night air when he took my right hand in both of his.

It made me nervous to be staring so directly into a stranger's eyes, but I felt immediately like this tension was something he intended, and I didn't want to spoil it by looking away. Still facing him in the doorway, I took one step back and to the side.

"Would you like to come in?"

Marcus followed me up the stairs in silence, walking a couple of steps behind me, even though his longer legs could have outpaced me easily. I knew he was watching me, and I felt a jolt of excitement at the idea of being looked at so penetratingly once I took my clothes off. Contrary to what I would have thought before getting into this business, the experience of being examined when I was in my most vulnerable state made me feel less, not more, self-conscious about my body. It was some weird form of validation for me—*If he's not looking away or asking for his money back, I must not be as unfortunate-looking as I feel when surrounded by the Skinny Big-Boobs Brigade of L.A. outside of session.*

Speaking of his money, it was the first time I would be dealing directly with such matters myself. Although I hadn't asked Catherine about it, I'd seen enough hooker scenes in movies to know that self-employed sex workers were supposed to get the money up front, no exceptions. As Marcus sat down on the edge of the bondage bed, I tried to think of the least tacky way to phrase my request.

"Are you nervous, Marnie?" A half-smile played on his lips as he crossed his legs and cupped one knee with interlaced fingers.

"Yes," I answered honestly.

"Why don't you take off your shoes and come sit next to me for a minute to relax."

I wasn't sure how getting closer to him right then was supposed to make me less nervous, but I nodded automatically and knelt down to untie my right shoe, anyway. Abruptly I let go of my shoelace and stood back up to face him.

"I'm sorry, but I'm supposed to pay the rent for the room before I start the session. Is that okay?"

It had just occurred to me that being in someone else's place was the perfect excuse for asking about the money. My clients wouldn't be talking to Catherine directly, and wouldn't know that she hadn't set down such a policy about the rent; I could take care of business while still appearing totally submissive.

"That's fine. Why don't you take this," Marcus reached into the front pocket of his shirt and pulled out a wad of money, "and leave your shoes and socks outside the door when you come back."

"Yes, sir," I took the money and went out into the hall.

I had put a large paper bag inside the room before Marcus got there, and had set my purse outside near the bathroom at the other end of the hallway. I went to it and stowed the money in one of the inside pockets, then waited a few moments to make it seem like I was spending time doing what I'd said I was going to do—pay Catherine. I knew I'd see her afterward and didn't want to interrupt now in case she was getting a pedicure or something from her slave.

The paper bag had a towel and a large glass bowl inside, the two items Marcus had instructed me to bring. I wasn't sure which of the implements hanging on the walls might come into play as well, but was less worried about them. The bowl was for me to squat over and pee in toward the end of the session. I assumed the towel was for me to kneel on or something. Or maybe he was going to jerk off and wanted something softer than a scratchy paper towel to finish in? I returned to the room, my feet bare as instructed, and looked at Marcus for a sign of what I was supposed to do next.

"Come stand here." Marcus pointed to a spot in front of him.

Planting myself there, I could feel his eyes on me again, but I kept my own gaze fixed on the floor between us. I was wound so tightly by that point, I couldn't really take any more of the staring contest.

"Take off your clothes, Marnie."

Reaching down, I unbuttoned my jeans and pulled them past my naked hips. I'd figured it would be more time-efficient to skip underwear.

"Turn around and bend over," he said, before I could pull off my T-shirt and bra.

Taking more deep breaths, I turned around and dropped my torso toward the floor, keeping my bare legs straight. I heard the sigh of the leather mattress as Marcus stood up, and seconds later felt his still-cool fingers brush my lower back.

"Grab your cheeks and hold yourself open for me."

I knew on some level that this type of pose was meant to embarrass me, to make me feel exposed in a way that would leave me more susceptible to whatever kinds of control he wanted to exert over me. But as his index finger stroked the delicate skin where my hands pulled me apart, I felt not humiliated but relieved. When he pushed on my opening like it was a button, I gasped and stood up halfway but kept my hands in place. I had wanted to be touched all over for so long, it seemed like. I would have kissed Marcus's feet then if he'd asked me to.

"Stand up, Marnie, and take off the rest of your clothes."

I turned around and did as he said, and when my shoulders were bare he rested his hands on them.

"You're doing very well. How are you feeling right now?"

"Thank you, sir. And I think I'm more relaxed," I said, as he massaged the leftover tension out of my back and upper arms.

"Good. I'd like you to stay that way. Come over here with me."

Marcus turned me around and took my hand, leading me over to the wooden stocks. Instead of opening them and having me put my head and wrists through the holes, he placed my hands on top of the closed apparatus and pulled my hips back so that my ass jutted out behind me.

I heard him walking to the other side of the room and wondered which of the implements he would be using on me. The room was silent for a moment, and then Marcus was coming back toward me. It sounded like he was tapping a pencil against his palm. *Is he going to write something before the flogging?*

"Have you ever been caned, Marnie?"

I turned my head to see him standing near my left side, holding a long, thin rattan cane in one hand.

"No, sir, I haven't," I said.

I had heard while working at the Dominion that the cane was a scary and dangerous tool for corporal punishment—scary because even a light caning could hurt like hell, and dangerous because bad aim on the part of the caner could result in things like nerve damage for the caned. I considered whether to tell Marcus that I wasn't up for it, but changed my mind when he started tapping it lightly up and down my cheeks. The rhythmic touch soothed away the anxiety that had cropped up moments before. I pushed my hips toward the cane and let my hands on the stocks hold the weight of my upper body as Marcus continued his soft drumming on my skin. When he stopped abruptly a few minutes later, I thought he was going to take me back to where I'd put the glass bowl and ask me to fill it. I was relieved that I really had to pee by that point.

"Now that I've warmed you up a bit, we're going to start. I want you to pick a number between one and ten."

I knew that whatever number I picked was going to be the number of cane strokes he gave me, but I didn't know how he expected me to make that choice without having any idea of what I was signing on for. Were they going to be just slightly harder than what he'd been doing so far, and hence something I could take at least ten of? Or was it going to be a full-fledged whacking, in which case I would want to opt for as few strokes as possible? I still hesitated to come across as a lightweight, and reminded myself that probably nothing Marcus did with the cane could hurt more than many of the things T had done without it.

"Seven?" I finally answered.

"Good."

Marcus ran the tip of the cane up and down the middle of my back. I dropped my head down between my shoulders and closed my eyes, shivering from a slight draft I began to feel now that we were closer to the windows. Marcus put a hand on the lower part of my back while his other hand made swishing noises with the cane behind me. *He can't possibly intend to hit me hard enough to generate that same noise for seven strokes, can he?*

"Is it okay if we have a safe word, sir?"

I hadn't thought before now to talk to him about how to bring things to a halt if I suddenly felt like I couldn't take what was going on. If someone didn't ask me about heavier play beforehand, it rarely occurred to me that a safe word might be necessary.

Are you afraid you might need it?" His tone was neutral as he asked the question.

I didn't want him to think that I was planning to pull the plug at the slightest discomfort, but I didn't want to lie to him, either.

"Yes. I am."

He took his hand off my back and must have put the cane on the soft bondage table, as I didn't hear him drop it. But suddenly both his hands were free, his ten fingers trailing up and down my bare back as he stood behind me.

"You're afraid it's going to hurt?" he leaned in and whispered in my ear.

*He smells like a . . . sexy . . . clean . . . forest.* I guessed there was no such thing as "Sexy Forest" cologne for men, but if Marcus ever bottled how he smelled that night, I would have bought it for every other man I got close enough to smell from then on.

"I think . . . I'm just scared because I don't know *what* it'll feel like," I finally answered.

"Would you like me to tell you?" One of his index fingers traced a large M between my shoulders.

"Yes, please."

"It's going to hurt in some way," he said dryly.

I laughed out loud then, knowing he was teasing me. I figured anyone with a sense of humor probably wasn't going to try to wipe the smile off my face with a brutal beating.

"Are you ready now, Marnie?"

"I think so."

"Ask me for it," Marcus's voice was soft, and the command sent a pleasurable chill up my spine.

"Would you . . . please . . . cane me now, sir?"

The first stroke slashed across the middle of both of my cheeks and left a thin line of fire that soaked through to the layers of flesh just under the surface and then disappeared altogether. I barely had time to gasp before the sensation was gone, and it was as if I'd never been struck in the first place.

"Wow, what was that?" I asked, genuinely startled.

"That was a fairly light stroke of the cane," Marcus answered. "Ask me for the next one."

I did as he said and felt the same thing, a centimeter lower. In addition to "scary" and "dangerous," someone should have also told me that caning was simply amazing. The sting of it was so intense when the cane landed, even for these supposedly light strokes, but it left not even a ghost of an impression mere seconds later.

"I want you to relax your shoulders," he said several minutes later. "Relax your whole body, as much as possible now. I'm going to cane you harder, and the less tense you are when this next stroke lands, the better it will feel. Ask me for it when you're ready."

His announcement excited and alarmed me. How do you relax when you hear something like that? And how could I not, now that he'd ordered me to? I took in deep breaths and forced my shoulders to drop back down, let my jaw release, and finally spoke in a steady voice.

"Would you please cane me again, sir?"

"It would be my pleasure," he said, and this time there was a faint whistle in the air before the implement landed on my skin.

I had just enough time to think *this is the feeling people are scared of* and to notice that I wasn't feeling scared of the pain yet myself when the second hard stroke cut across my ass just slightly above the previous one. I cried out and gripped the stocks, pressing my forehead into the slightly cool stretch of wood between my hands.

"That was excellent, Marnie."

Marcus let the cane fall to the floor and came up quickly behind me, pushing one of his legs between mine and rubbing my still-burning skin with his hands. I pushed back and dropped down a little so that his thigh could press more firmly into me. I could feel myself swelling down there and was surprised when it was accompanied by a real craving for more strokes of the cane. It had stung so much, but now that the pain had mostly vanished again, my skin ached for more of it.

I had never really believed T when he'd said that I was a serious masochist, that I liked intense pain. If anything, I thought he just said it to try and convince me it was true, like the power of suggestion and repetition in advertising. Even when I'd played heavily with Phil, the combination of his touch and my excitement had rendered the floggings virtually painless. I could not remember ever having felt something that hurt enough to make me yell and then having a desire to feel more of it as soon as possible. I felt a sort of narcissistic awe, in that instant, at the idea that I might be turning into something different from what I had been up to that point. Could experience and the right person make you feel pain as pain and like it anyway? What kind of voodoo was *that?*

"Stand up."

Marcus put a hand around my waist and pulled me into an upright position. Keeping his leg between mine, he rubbed my shoulders yet again and pressed soothing fingers into the back of my neck. I thought I could doze off right there on my feet.

"I'd like to finish up tonight by having you at least *hover* over the bowl, even if that's as far as it gets."

Marcus moved his leg and I turned around to face him. The clock on the far wall said that our time was almost up. I could hardly believe it. I started to feel nervous again, uptight even, and finally realized that I hadn't really given much thought to this peeing scene up to now. It had sounded so harmless at first mention that I'd mostly put it out of my mind. Now I wondered—was it supposed to truly embarrass me? And if that was the point, why was I going along with it? I didn't do humiliation scenes, and as much as I liked Marcus, I didn't want to make an exception for him. I knew I had to say something.

"Sir, can I ask you why you want me to do this?"

I watched while Marcus brought a straight-backed chair from the side of the room into the middle and placed the large glass bowl a couple of feet in front of it.

"*Why?*" Marcus repeated my question, and looked at me with sincere surprise.

"Yeah, I mean . . . are you going to make fun of me, or . . ."

"Make *fun* of you? Certainly not. No. That's not what I had in mind at all," he said, confused.

"Okay," I sighed with relief. "I got afraid for a minute that this was some type of humiliation scene. It sort of seems like it, and I haven't done anything like this before."

"Well, of course, in a sense it is, but there are many kinds of humiliation scenes, Marnie."

Marcus sat in the chair and motioned me over. I stood in front of him, straddling the empty bowl, and he took my hands.

"Some things that fall under the humiliation category are more about vulnerability than degradation—stripping you bare, so to speak, and forcing you to be fully exposed in front of me. Can you think of a more helpless situation than being made to look in my eyes while I watch you now?"

"I'm not sure."

"Do you not want to expose yourself to me completely?"

It sounded like a real question, not a scripted prompt for the "right" answer, and I thought about it. At the mere sound of his voice, my body wanted to open itself entirely to whatever he wanted to do with me. But this peeing-in-a-bowl thing was so obviously not about just my body.

"I don't know if it's something I want or not, because I don't know if I'll like how it feels yet."

"Well, would you like to try it and see? If you find that you hate it, you always have your safe word," he said, still holding my hands between us.

"Incidentally, what *is* my safe word, sir?"

"Let's use *mercy,* for simplicity's sake."

"Thank you," I said, and lowered myself over the bowl when he nodded toward it.

It didn't feel as odd or as ridiculous as I had expected it to. Maybe peeing in a bowl in front of someone who wants to see it just isn't such a big, dramatic deal after all. I started to feel the space around me dissolve as my concentration whittled down to the man sitting in front of me, the feel of his hands on mine, and the muscles that needed to unclench in order for me to pull this off. And then it was just coming out of me, a stream of liquid making a soft hiss that echoed inside the bowl, almost clear because of all the water I had drunk before the session. Marcus and I smiled at each other for several seconds, and then I looked away and laughed. We were both so pleased with me you'd have thought I'd just graduated from college or something.

After I finished, Marcus helped me stand back up, and took the towel off the nearby bondage bed. Slowly, he patted the insides of my thighs, then pressed the still-folded towel between my legs, holding it firm as I put my hands on his shoulders and leaned into him. We stayed that way for a couple of minutes, my hips rocking slightly to make the pressure between my legs vary between *nice* and *very nice.*

"I better start getting dressed," I finally whispered into his neck, and he put a hand around my waist to keep me from going anywhere for another few seconds, then let me go.

# EIGHT

**"MA'AM? IS YOUR** name on the list?" A man not much taller than I am but with considerably more hair on his chest, was staring at me, pen in one hand and stapled sheets of rumpled paper in the other. It was the second time he'd asked the question. I had been so distracted in trying to focus my gaze on anything except his naked balls that I hadn't answered the first time.

"Sorry—I should be on there, yes. Marnie. I just started renting from Catherine last week."

In the days that followed my first session with Marcus, I had gotten several e-mails but no real prospects for more work. A few people had written to say they would be in Los Angeles some time in the future; two had specified needing to come on my face at the end of the session; and one had wanted to know whether he could come over and do my dishes in exchange for getting a spanking from *me* afterwards. Of all the useless correspondence that week, his had irritated me the most. From what I could see online and in the one print magazine where kinky professionals advertised, there had to be more than a hundred dominatrixes in L.A., and yet this wannabe houseboy had managed to direct his *services offered* e-mail to the one and only professional submissive. How could someone that inattentive be good at housework?

Also annoying was my financial situation. I wasn't quite out of money yet, but found the pace of two hundred dollars a week take-home worrisome. I had called Catherine to ask for advice about how else to reach a good client base. She had told me about a play party she was having this evening, where most of the attendees would be submissive men, but where a potential dominant client did occasionally show up. I'd never been to a play party and was curious. It had to beat the hell out of sitting in my apartment waiting for another e-mail or phone call.

"Ah, here," the naked man nodded, and drew a line through some faint type on the list he was holding. "I think Catherine's in one of the back rooms if you want to go say hello. All the ladies are welcome to change and store their street clothes in the front bathroom around the corner."

"Thank you," I said, and moved past him into the hallway.

I passed two more nude guys and then nearly bumped into a third as he came around the corner of the open bathroom when I was about to step into it.

"Oh!" I said.

"Sorry. Didn't mean to scare you," the man said sheepishly, and moved in the same direction I did when I attempted to let him pass.

We moved back in the opposite direction together immediately, and it was all I could do not to hold my purse out in front of me at the exact height of his private parts. He had come within inches of nailing me in the stomach with his wild thatch of pubic hair. I'm all for new experiences, but a woman has her limits.

"I'm just gonna stand here for a second," I said politely, and was grateful when he carefully stepped the other way so each of us could move forward.

The sight of pairs and small groups of naked men chatting casually throughout the length of the hall was causing a bit of a sensory over-load. I saw women in fetish garb joining in some of the conversations, and heard the distinct sound of asses being whacked outside of view, but, in general, this party seemed to me, so far, to be little more than an old-fashioned social for naked, middle-aged men.

I closed the bathroom door behind me and set my purse and bag of sex clothes on a shelf of towels. I had brought a new outfit with me—a lacy black push up bra that made me look a full cup size larger, and matching see-through lace short shorts, with a middle seam that just barely covered my own parts in front. After pulling on the requisite black thigh-highs and four-inch heels, I stashed my purse and street clothes in the larger bag and stuffed it all in a cor-ner behind a wicker laundry basket.

"Oops!" A beautiful black-haired woman opened the bath-room door. "Need something out of my bag," she said, smiling.

"That's okay, I'm pretty much done in here."

The bathroom was big enough for three or four people to stand around in comfortably, and, as the stranger moved to the far end to search through what looked like a doctor's bag, I took in the rest of her. She was wearing what had to be seven-inch heels, so I guessed she was actually closer to my height than she'd first seemed. She had a petite frame, but her outfit made her look taller—thigh-high stockings, high-cut leather thong, full leather corset that pulled her into an exaggerated hourglass shape and fit snugly under her leather push up bra. Her straight hair fell to the middle of her back, cov-ering much of her smooth, light almond skin.

"I'm Mistress K."

She held out a slender hand with long red nails, facing me again after fishing a large purple flogger from her bag.

"I'm Marnie." I shook her hand. "I do sub sessions. Nice to meet you."

K cocked her head and grinned at me. "It's a pleasure." She held onto me a few seconds longer. "I haven't met a lot of pro subs. How long have you been working?"

"I started at the Dominion a couple of months ago but just went out on my own as of last week, really. I'm renting space here for my sessions. Do you work out of here as well?"

K turned abruptly at the sound of people coming toward us. A man wearing a collar and leash was being led noisily down the hall by a tall blonde woman in a bright red catsuit and platform boots.

"I'm going to piss all over you, slave boy! Now get in that tub and be a good toilet!" the woman barked. "'Scuse us, ladies," she nodded toward K and pulled her captive into the restroom.

K and I stepped quickly out into the hall. I looked at the flogger dangling from K's hand and suddenly felt self-conscious about having started a conversation.

"You're probably in the middle of something. I don't mean to keep you," I offered politely.

"I wasn't actually," she smiled, "but I am now. Let's go find a quieter place to talk."

She waved me toward her with a quick motion of her hand, and I followed her to the back of the loft.

"Perfect. Let's go in here," she said a few seconds later, having found the room I'd played in with Marcus empty.

She closed the door behind us and used the pad of her thumb and the side of her index finger to turn the lock on the doorknob. I wondered how long it took a person to learn to do things without the easy use of her fingertips from all those nails. K sat in the large, throne-like chair against the wall and motioned for me to make myself comfortable on the bondage bed.

"In answer to your question, I just started renting from Catherine myself."

"She's really cool. I meant to go say hi to her, but I'm relieved that I got sidetracked. I'm not sure I know how to successfully navigate all those bobbing male parts in the crowd just yet," I said.

K laughed. "Yeah, you get used to it after a while. I guess your clients don't get naked as often as ours do. Anyway, I don't think Catherine will miss you for a while. Last I saw her, she was knee-deep in a heavy caning and piercing scene across the hall."

I nodded, and we were both quiet for a few seconds.

"Have you been doing this a long time, or is that too personal to ask?" I finally blurted.

K waved the notion off. "Nothing's too personal. I've been doing this for a few years professionally, and a couple of years before that in my personal life."

She stood up and, eyeing the implements hanging on the nearest wall, approached the shelves and hooks and began fingering various items on each.

"So tell me about you," she said, inspecting a set of leather wrist cuffs.

"Hm. I don't know," I said, uncrossing my legs. Pushing the straps of my heels off with my toes, I pulled my feet up onto the bondage bed and sat Indian style, my hands folded in my lap. "I guess I feel a little weird still. I mean I don't know if I'm used to all of this yet."

K turned to look at me, eyebrows raised.

"The work, you mean, or . . . ?"

"I guess I thought that because I'm seriously into the scene, I'd get bombarded with grateful clients right off the bat, you know? But things have been kind of slow so far. Even the clients who seem to like me a lot don't book me as often as I'd thought people would."

K came to sit on another corner of the bondage bed.

"The uncertainty of sessions and income does take some getting used to. Someone might really love playing with you, but only be able to afford to see you once a month, or even less. Some of them will see you once a week for months, and then suddenly disappear. And some of *those* guys will resurface again years later."

"Damn!" I said. "It's so hard not to get my hopes up, especially when I really like a client. How long does it take to build up enough of these rotating, sometimes disappearing clients so that you don't end up bankrupt?"

K laughed. "You're not gonna go bankrupt. Of course I don't know you, but if you're as into it as you seem, you're certainly attractive enough, and subs are certainly in demand enough, that you should be fine. And after you've played with enough great clients, you'll get more confidence around the idea that more are always on the way. You won't feel so attached to every single one who makes you quiver."

"God, I hope that happens soon," I sighed. I'd been obsessively checking my in-box for an e-mail from Marcus ever since the night we'd met.

"And one thing you can do in the meantime is to play as much as you want to outside of sessions as well. Are you seeing anyone in your personal life?"

"No," I said simply, fighting the urge to add *not right now* so that it wouldn't sound so absolute.

K nodded thoughtfully. "That doesn't mean you're out of options." She got up and stood in front of me. "For instance, you could play with selective partners at parties like this. I, for one, would love to play with a sub like you."

Her invitation didn't exactly startle me, as I'd felt some kind of *something* going on between us since we'd first locked eyes in the bathroom. I looked at her beautiful face—blood-red lips, the same olive skin as on her bare arms and back, and wide-set, almond-shaped eyes framed with velvety, thick lashes—and knew I wanted to accept. Still, I had some nervousness about playing with her. What if I got attached to *her* just like I'd gotten attached to Marcus and others? I knew she'd be great at it—she made a living convincing men to shell out thousands of dollars a year to suffer at her hands.

"You look a little hesitant. Perhaps it's too sudden for you," she began apologetically.

"No, no, it's not that," I interrupted. "I would . . . very much like to play with you. I'm just afraid it'll make me feel attracted to you," I said quickly, staring at my hands, "and I don't want that to end up being a weird thing."

K brushed a strand of hair from my face. "I'm not worried about it." She went to the door and spoke to me as she opened it. "I'm going to grab a couple of other toys from my bag, and I'd like you to prepare yourself for me while I'm gone. You may keep your shoes off, and I'd like you to remove your bra as well. I'll leave it up to you whether to completely undress or not."

As soon as she left, I unhooked my bra and slid the heavy cups off my now slightly vibrating frame. I could tell instantly that K was right. I *did* feel better now that I was about to get to play with someone again. I guess, before then, I'd just thought that it was either wait around for sessions, which sucked when business was slow, or try to drum up some kinky one-night stands at clubs or online, to tide me over until I met someone I wanted to date. I'd figured one-night stands would leave me lonely if they were good, and would be a waste of time if they were bad. Catherine had these parties once a month. Maybe I could come every time and play with K—and who knew what might happen?

I wasn't sure what exactly she had meant by telling me to prepare myself, so I got back on the bondage table and simply knelt down, waiting. When I heard the door open, I put my hands behind my back, thrust out my chest, and sucked in my stomach. Whatever the hell was going on, I at least wanted to look good for it.

"Nice, Marnie," she said in a low voice, and ran a fingernail along the base of my throat to my belly button.

Her other hand held the same purple flogger and some kind of metal chain with things that looked like internal clock parts attached to each end. She placed the items next to me on the bed.

"Kiss my hand."

She held out the back of her hand and I leaned forward to kiss it. Her skin was silky and smelled of some sort of perfumed lotion. I wondered fleetingly if I would be able to smell her on me at all after we were done. K stepped in close and lifted her knee up onto the bed, to push my legs open wider. I could smell her hair conditioner (an expensive salon brand), her perfume (a delicate scent that made me think of orchids), and even her deodorant (Secret, Shower Fresh scent, same as what I used). I inhaled deeply as she put her hands on me and began a slow massage.

Starting at my shoulders, she ran the tips of her fingernails down the length of my arms several times, first down the middle and over the backs of my hands, then dragging them lightly through the inside crook of each arm. Her touch and the intoxicating smells pulsing off her with each movement began to lull me into a state of relaxation that was new to me. When she moved her hands inward to stroke and circle my breasts, I shivered.

"How are you feeling right now?"

K took each of my nipples between her slender fingers and began to pinch and pull rhythmically.

"Excellent, thank you, Mistress."

"Good," she let her hands drop and stepped away. "I want you to lean your head back now, and push your chest out for me."

She picked up the leather flogger and ran a hand through the strands to straighten them. I did as she asked, and shut my eyes. A second later, the flogger landed with a gentle thud across my right breast. It felt soothing in much the same way her hands had, with an extra tingling from the light slap of the leather. I pushed my chest out farther, and heard K murmur her approval. She began alternating strokes between my right and left sides, working up from a completely painless level to a barely noticeable sting. I don't know how long she worked on my breasts, but eventually I felt her hand behind my head instead of the flogger on my chest.

"You can bring your head back now, but open your legs a little more for me."

My neck was a little stiff when I opened my eyes to straighten myself, and K squeezed and rubbed the back of my neck when she saw me trying to loosen it.

"Mm, thank you Mistress," I said, and waited.

She swung the flogger between my legs, and I jumped when it landed. Not because it hurt, but just from the surprise of it. It was the softest of taps, and made me acutely aware of how aroused I had become when she'd been flogging my breasts. Everything had become swollen down there, so that even the least of sensations provoked an excruciatingly pleasurable response. K noticed when I pushed my hips slightly forward, and increased the tempo and intensity. I began to moan quietly, finding the space between the strokes almost unbearable as they landed increasing pressure on a part of me that was by that time aching for it. After a few minutes, she set the flogger aside and directed me to lie down on my back. I heard the jingling of that metal toy I'd seen earlier, and then K was playing again with my nipples.

"Have you ever had these kinds of clamps used on you before?"

She held up the silver chain by one of its ends, and squeezed open what I now understood to be a kind of nipple clamp. It looked like two interlocking circles, and when you pressed on one of them, the other parted to reveal small rubber pads to fit around whatever skin was clenched between.

"No, Mistress, I haven't. They look kind of neat, though. What are they?"

"They're called clover clamps, and they *are* neat," she smiled. "They're also pretty intense, Marnie. Would you be willing to try them for me?"

I expected to feel afraid from the sound of it, like I had been with Marcus when he'd been about to cane me for real and I hadn't known how bad it would hurt. But with K, I just had this feeling from the way she touched me that there was nothing she couldn't help guide my body pleasurably through. I felt also that she would be kind to me if I couldn't take it and had to ask her to stop. What did I have to lose?

"Yes, thank you for asking me," I finally answered.

She took my left nipple with her free hand and pulled it away from my body, drawing the skin out so that she could get as much of my nipple as possible into the clamp. She positioned the metal contraption around the base of my areola and slowly let it close with increasing pressure on my skin. By the time she let it go completely, and then subjected my other nipple to the same procedure, I was feeling a steady throb in each breast. The throbbing quickly turned into what felt like an unbearable ache.

"Mistress K," I gasped, "I'm not sure how much longer I can—"

"I understand," she interrupted. "I want you to feel yourself, feel your whole body now floating on top of the pain." She placed a cool hand on my bare stomach. "The sting of it, the burning, it's all just waves of the ocean rolling under you as you stay afloat. Let it roll by. Feel yourself resting calmly above it."

She continued murmuring to me for several more minutes, coaxing and encouraging me to relax, to experience the clamps on my nipples as something besides a source of pain. Her voice and her soft hands elsewhere on my body made it easy for me to close my eyes and picture exactly what she was describing. The sensation in my breasts started to feel like something I had a hold of, instead of something that had a hold of me, and I imagined water supporting my naked body, with warm, gentle waves beneath me. I breathed in as deeply as I could, and it began to seem like there were moments when I felt almost nothing in my breasts at all. After several more minutes, K announced that the clamps were coming off.

"The blood rushes back in when they're first removed, and it actually hurts a lot more in that second than it does to keep them on indefinitely. I want you to breathe in deeply when I tell you to, and concentrate on continuing to breathe. It will help with the pain just like my voice was helping you before."

She counted to three and took the clamp off my right nipple. I yelled in pain and surprise, but kept breathing. She was right. It immediately helped the sharp pain soften into something bearable before it disappeared altogether within seconds. Knowing what to expect after the first one, I was scared to have the second one removed, but again it was over almost before I knew it. It reminded me a little of the caning with Marcus, the way something so intense could come and go so quickly.

"I'd like to finish with some more flogging. Do you think you can handle that?"

I didn't think I could handle *not* being flogged some more right then, so I nodded silently and let K help me up off my back. She had me get on my knees again on the bed, with my legs spread, and my hands clasped behind my neck.

"You can use *mercy* as your safe word if you need it." She leaned over to whisper in my ear.

I smiled and closed my eyes; I couldn't imagine ever wanting, much less needing, her to stop anything she chose to do with my body by that point. When she started to swing the flogger between my legs again repeatedly, I leaned my head back and let out a deep breath.

As K slowly increased the force behind each successive stroke, I started to get confused about what I was feeling. The harder the whip landed, the harder I *needed* it to land. I wanted more and constant pressure, once the initial rhythmic weight of the flogger got me so aroused. But the more K flogged me and the more I craved, the more it started to really hurt as well. Because it stung and felt so great all in the same instant, each time the flogger landed, I got nervous about what we were doing. What if I got into such a frenzy that I needed it to go on until I reached orgasm? Would that be too overtly sexual a response to have with this woman I barely knew? Was it even *possible* to have an orgasm this way? I'd only been able to come with my hand up to that point, and, on very rare occasions, someone else's mouth. What if it took so much flogging for me to come this way that by the time I reached a climax, I had accidentally let myself get damaged? I looked up to see K concentrating on the swing of her arm, breathing hard from the work of flogging me so thoroughly. I was panting by that point as well, and had the overwhelming urge to beg her—I didn't know for what.

"*Please,* Mistress," I finally moaned, my head spinning with irrational visions of explosive pleasure and broken clitorises.

K immediately eased up, and I immediately regretted it. It wasn't enough, this suddenly lighter flogging, but I didn't want to be pushy by asking her to do anything differently.

"You okay?" She looked into my eyes, swinging the leather strands slowly at my open legs as she asked the question.

I sucked in a huge breath. "*Definitely,*" I sighed. "I didn't want you to have to stop on my account, I just got scared. But I would have said the safe word if I'd needed—"

"I know," she smiled. "It's okay. I didn't want to push you too hard. After all, we just met."

She set down the flogger and put a reassuring hand on my shoulder.

"Thank you," I nodded, feeling simultaneously happy and frustrated.

I already missed what she'd been doing minutes before, but I liked that she seemed to be almost more protective of me than I was. She sat across from me in the throne chair again, and I lay down on my stomach to rest.

"That was so nice," I said dreamily, and somehow my stating the obvious like that made us both laugh.

"You're such a *beautiful* masochist," K grinned. "God, your skin is like silk!"

I felt the familiar heat in my face and neck and thanked her without meeting her eyes.

"So was the Dominion your first experience with submission?"

"For some reason, it almost feels like it. It's all been so different from what I did before. But no, it wasn't my first time. I was in a relationship a few months ago with an older, experienced domme. After I broke up with him, I had a hard time meeting anyone else to play with, or at least anyone I liked. I finally went to the Dominion out of physical desperation."

"Yeah," K said dryly, "I'm glad I'm not a sub, having to deal with all the egos of male doms [when referring to male dominants, it's dom(s) and female is domme(s)] out there."

"Why is that, anyway?" I asked. "I mean, you and Catherine are two of the most dominant people I've met, and neither of you acts all cartoonish about it. Why are the men so different?"

"Partly, it's cultural, I think. We're dommes, but we're still women. We're socialized to care about our partners' well being even while we're torturing them," she laughed. "But to be fair, Marnie, I've definitely met a lot of amazing dominant men in the scene. It's not that different from dating in the vanilla world. It just takes time to meet the right person."

I knew she was right. I hadn't really looked beyond Internet chat rooms and that one Threshold meeting, neither of which was necessarily a true representation of the kink scene at large. Still, I was relieved not to be as concerned with finding a personal relationship as I used to be.

K leaned forward in her chair abruptly. "Hey, speaking of the time it takes to meet the right person, I have a proposition for you."

"Whatever it is, if it's a proposition from you, the answer's yes," I said, knowing that while this sounded like a flirty line, I meant every word of it. "Okay, seriously, I'm listening."

"Well, I have this wonderful playmate in New York who wants to session with a female sub. I keep telling him I'll bring someone, but I haven't been that impressed with the pro subs I've met so far. You don't have to answer now, but I was wondering if you might consider it?"

I was quiet for a second, excited by this sudden turn of events, but unsure of how it might actually take place.

"It sounds like fun, but I don't know that I could afford the trip."

"You don't need to *afford* it, Marnie!" She rolled her eyes. "Everything will be taken care of. Plus, you might even get more sessions on your own while you're in town. There are some pretty amazing players back east who I'm sure would bombard you with session requests. The scene's different there. You'll absolutely stand out."

*Stand out.* With how slow things had been at home lately, I couldn't have imagined anything better at that point than a paid vacation where I got to feel like a star even for a couple of days.

"So, what would the session be like, and how many hours would I need to play to settle up with whoever's covering my expenses?"

K surprised me by laughing again. "It doesn't work like that. You'll be getting paid your normal fee for the session with my friend, and you're not responsible for paying anyone back for the expense of getting you there."

I couldn't believe it. Travel, more playing with K and some guy she liked, and the chance to establish even a fledgling client base in New York City? Rich perverts tended to get around. I guessed it could even increase my business at home if I got to know clients from other parts of the country who traveled. There was only one thing I was worried about.

"So, I don't want to look a gift horse in the mouth, but I sort of need a lot of privacy and stuff or I get stressed out . . ."

I didn't know what to expect about sleeping and bathroom arrangements for the trip.

"Oh you'll have your own accommodations, of course! He usually puts me up at the Mercer and stays there with me for most of the trip, and you would be set up nearby in your own place."

I knew things were moving really fast, and that the conservative approach would be to at least talk to Catherine before answering. I also knew that my gut feelings had so far proven more reliable in my life than other people's opinions. If I had to learn to weather the downsides of this business—like slow times, crushes that couldn't be returned, and the occasional lame client—it seemed only right that I should take full advantage of the upside. Right now that upside was standing in front of me, holding out a virtual plane ticket with lodging in her sensually talented hands.

"Is there anything in particular I should bring with me? I've never been to New York City before."

# NINE

**THE FIRST THING** I noticed, and liked, about being in New York City was the smell. Actually, it was the smell of the ride between Newark airport and Manhattan that first got me—a mixture, like the landscape, of concrete/metal/industrial stuff and of lush green trees, of forests even. It was everything I had not grown up with in the suburbs of Los Angeles: real city and real country both.

I was supposed to meet K at her hotel in SoHo, and she was going to take me down the street to the little studio apartment she'd rented for me for three nights. She had found it through an agency in New York that specialized in short-term sublets. When I got off the plane, I'd found a voice mail from her saying that she would be in session until a little later than my arrival time, but had left the keys for me in an envelope at the front desk of her hotel. When the driver let me off at the intersection of Prince and Mercer, I got a look at the street and had to suppress the urge to clutch my heart and say *Awww.* The ground beneath my feet was more cobblestone than dark pavement.

The lobby of the Mercer Hotel opened into the hotel's bar and restaurant, which was noisy and full even at this early hour. The clock behind the front desk clerk said it was five thirty p.m. When I opened the envelope K had left for me, it contained a little hand-printed map to my place, two keys, and a note that said she would come find me around six. It also contained two hundred and fifty dollars in cash. The note said nothing about the money, and I won-dered if it was an advance on the session we'd be doing, or a short term loan since she knew I was pretty broke. Whatever it was, it felt like a windfall. Although K was younger than me by a few years, I had started thinking of her as my fairy godmother.

The little sublet was dreamy—one big room plus a bathroom, with a little slash of a kitchen off to one side near the front door. The bed was high and covered in soft sheets and an afghan; the mid-dle of the room was decked out like a bona fide *parlor* of all things, with a small liquor stand near the stiff old couch and art deco cof-fee table. The entire kitchen took up just slightly more space than my writing desk at home, with a vintage Sears refrigerator that was about fifty percent narrower than normal but still a good five inches taller than me—kind of like the women I'd seen between K's hotel and this apartment building.

Before I could get my shampoo and make-up neatly laid out in the tiny, clean bathroom, my cell phone rang. Fifteen minutes later, I had booked two spanking sessions for the following day and night at a local dungeon that allowed visiting pros to rent from them by the hour. Both the clients were regulars at the place, and had booking privileges with the receptionist. I wouldn't have to do any-thing but call the next day on my way over to confirm. My phone rang a third time, and I was about to ask the caller to try me again the next morning when I recognized the number as K's.

"Welcome to the city! How do you like your place?"

K smiled and raised her water glass at me. She had met me outside the apartment building and steered us toward a cozy Italian restaurant a little after six, as promised.

"It's so cute. Thank you! This whole little neighborhood is great. I love New York so much already!" I whispered excitedly, not wanting the people at nearby tables to think I was a geeky tourist.

K laughed. "You're welcome. I'm so glad you like it. I thought you would. I stayed there during my last trip. My client was thinking about getting me an ongoing sublet instead of continuing to stash me at the Mercer, since my trips are getting longer each time."

"The Mercer's gorgeous," I said, still impressed by its understated elegance, but secretly pleased that I was in the unintimidating little sublet with its view of the tree-lined street below.

"You're welcome to come by any time," K said. I'll be out a lot doing sessions, so you can either come to the room and order room service or you can come over to the restaurant whenever you're hungry and charge it to my account."

"Wow, that's really kind of you, but I know that's expensive— plus I think I can manage off the money you left me. Which I want to thank you for, by the way," I said.

She waved her hand, as if I were making a big deal out of her loaning me a quarter for a phone call.

"So, I mean, can I pay you back from the money I make while I'm here? I already have two sessions lined up for tomorrow," I offered.

"No. There's no paying it back. It's for you."

The look on her face was like I'd seen on my dad's and his friend's faces when they used to fight bitterly over who was going to pick up the check at dinner. They would literally get furious with each other over the right to be generous every single time. I never understood why people got genuinely mad at each other because of an equal desire to treat each other nicely, but I knew I didn't want to get into such a struggle with K. Aside from not wanting to annoy her, I also really liked the feeling of being taken care of so thoroughly. I felt like I'd been barely succeeding in taking care of myself at home, what with still struggling to get my new business off the ground.

"Thank you, then, again."

K shook her head once, quickly, while staring into her water glass. A few seconds of awkward silence followed. I began to worry that I had insulted her, despite my best efforts not to. The only thing I could tell for sure was that it would be a great idea to change the subject.

"So I have two people who want to see me tomorrow, one in the afternoon and one at night. You'd said things would be pretty flexible with your guy, but I wanted to see if I should set aside any time in particular."

I would only be in town for three nights, including this one, and didn't want to book myself out of being able to see the one person who'd made it possible for me to come here in the first place.

"He actually had to leave town. I just saw him for the last time this afternoon, so go ahead and schedule whatever else you want," she said without elaborating.

"Oh."

I was confused and also a little disappointed. I had thought we were going to do at least a couple hours of session time with him. I had been looking forward to being in K's hands again, and to the adventure of doing a double session with this man she seemed to have a particularly close professional relationship with. But there was something closed off in K's expression now, and I could tell it would be better not to ask for an explanation.

After dinner, K made me promise to check in with her every day, and to call her or come by her room if I needed anything, including just someone to talk to. She put her arm around my shoulder on the way out of the restaurant.

"I know you have a good head on your shoulders, and this is a great town, I just don't want you to be running around here without a safety net."

"Yes, Mother," I said to tease her, but her fussing made me feel somehow sublimely protected and free at the same time.

She hugged me good night like we were long-lost friends as we moved to go our separate ways on the street. I watched her for a few seconds as she glided away, her back straight, heels clicking briskly on the sidewalk. I half-expected to see her dissolve into a cloud of colorful sparkles and a small *ping!* before she made it to the next block.

The dungeon was in a ten-story office building near the Empire State Building. I had to buzz an intercom from the lobby in order even to get on the elevator, let alone get off at the right floor—there were no call buttons in the lobby. The elevator wouldn't go to the ground floor unless one of the building's inhabitants sent it there. When I got in, the sixth-floor button was already lit up. Although it seemed obvious that it worked the same way for the other businesses here as well, I did think it was kind of a nice touch for a dungeon, imagining some all-powerful elevator goddess controlling the whole thing from above. Instead of opening onto a hallway, the small, slow car let me out into what was essentially a cage with a doorbell inside it. As the elevator doors closed behind me, I could see through the heavy screen door in front of me to a lobby with deep red walls and dark oak furniture. A severe-looking blond woman sat behind a desk and did not look up. I pressed the small button on the wall in front of me, and it rang loudly on the other side. The blond receptionist raised her head.

"Yes?"

"Hi, I'm Marnie, I have a couple of sessions booked here today?"

The question in my voice irritated me. I had meant to arrive here all guarded and sure of myself, prepared for a similarly competitive environment as what I'd left behind at the Dominion.

"Open the door when you hear the buzz."

I pulled the screen door open like she told me to and stood in front of her, waiting. Without looking at me or saying another word, the blond woman got up and vanished through an open door behind her desk.

*Now, what?* I didn't know if I was supposed to have a seat in one of the plush chairs facing the desk, follow her, or stand here at attention until further notice. Just as I was getting geared up to say a loud and accusatory *Hel-LO?* the receptionist re-appeared in the doorway with a pretty brunette woman behind her.

"Hi Marnie, I'm Ava. We spoke on the phone this morning. Let me show you where you can change your clothes and keep your stuff."

She smiled as she walked toward me, putting a hand on my shoulder when she reached me.

"Hi. Nice to meet you. Thanks for letting me rent here."

"You're quite welcome. It's pretty brave of you to come to Manhattan alone for sub sessions, I must say."

I shook my head. "Not brave at all, actually—a friend was really generous in bringing me here with her this time. Already I feel like I want to come back on my own, though."

I'd done a little research online and had only seen one other submissive who worked in New York at all, and it was only one week a month, when she took the train in from upstate. Her Web site said she saw clients at another one of the commercial dungeons in midtown, and did not meet people in hotel rooms. Although I hadn't done so yet either, I certainly planned to. Not only were hotel rooms a turn-on for me ever since T, but I loved the idea of keeping all the money myself instead of having to pay a rental fee.

"There are plenty of domme clients; you should do really well here," Ava said as we walked back through that same open door into a softly lit hallway.

As I followed her past a couple of closed doors and around a corner to a small room, I thought Ava was probably right. With no twenty-year-olds to compete with even at the "houses" out here, it seemed like I should be able to make a bundle. Maybe I could find out from K without being tacky just how much it had cost to bring me here this time. Ava ushered me in ahead of her.

"This is my private dressing room and office. I thought you'd be more comfortable here than trying to find space for your stuff in the main staff room."

I was a little shocked that this woman who didn't even know me was going to let me be alone in her private room. I wouldn't have been shocked once she *had* known me, but to treat me with such trust and respect before she could have known it was safe was amazing, I thought. Secretly, I wanted to believe that, unlike Hillary, for example, Ava had taken one look at me and decided I was an honest person.

"I have to get back to the books, but you can come find me or ask Mara at the desk if you need anything. The room you'll be using for your session is right next door to this one, and you let us know if you need us to take any special safety measures. Otherwise, we'll stay out of your hair."

Ava smiled again and closed the door behind her, leaving me in the slightly claustrophobic little room with its naked light bulb in the ceiling and shelf upon shelf of latex and leather clothing. There was a chair and makeup table with a large mirror on the wall in front of them. I set my things on the chair and leaned down to take off my shoes when the door opened again, barely missing my head.

"Oh, sorry. Is this your room? I thought Mistress Ava had said I could change in here," I said to the petite, lusciously curvy woman in the doorway. She had long, brown hair that hung in soft waves past her shoulders, and the sweetest face I'd ever seen on a domme, or maybe anywhere else.

"I'm Mistress Lissette. Ava and I are co-owners. And yes, this is my room as well. But there's no need for apology."

Her eyes widened slightly and she looked me pointedly up and down. She had a bit of an accent, but I couldn't tell if it was French or Spanish.

"Oh, okay. I'm Marnie, by the way, I'm renting space here," I said, and held out my hand.

"I know who you are, you little angel," she purred, and took my hand in both of hers, clasping it warmly. "I know exactly who you are! You're my birthday present." She turned her head and called into the hallway behind her. "Look at you, the perfect size! Just what I wanted. Turn around, let me see the rest of my present," she coaxed, her voice high in exaggerated anticipation.

I let Lissette's joking flirtation go straight to my head. First, I was given the VIP treatment with the private room, and now I was someone's little angel to boot. Where had New York City been all my life?

"Mara, come see what they got me for my birthday!" Lissette yelled again into the hallway. The blond receptionist poked her head around the corner.

"Cute," she nodded, sizing me up as if we hadn't met in the lobby a short while before.

"Adorable!" Lissette sang, cupping my face in her soft brown hands.

I went against my grain and let her hold my face instead of pulling away—it was her birthday after all—and when she finally left and shut the door behind her, pretending to lock it so that no one could come in and steal her "present," I missed her. It hit me that I'd be back in Los Angeles in less than forty-eight hours. I wished I could put my finger on some imaginary emergency stop button to make the time go by slower. I felt like I'd only just stepped off the plane at Newark, and it was getting so good, it was already awful to think I had only one more full day here after this one.

Pushing thoughts of returning home out of my mind, I pulled off the rest of my clothes and put on one of the no-longer-new leopard-print dresses I'd bought a couple of months earlier. They'd be fresh to my Manhattan clients, so I hadn't even bothered to go shopping before I'd left home. As I was finishing up with my stockings and some lipstick, there was a knock at the door and Lissette opened it a crack to whisper that my client had arrived. I thanked her and looked in the full-length mirror one last time before heading out to see what kind of kinky men the Big Apple had to offer.

What with the little office/dressing room and the little lobby, I wasn't surprised by the size of the room Ava had given me for my session. I *was* surprised by how unusually tan my client, John, was.

The map of lines on his face and neck indicated that his dark skin was something he'd been working on for years, not simply sprayed on hours before. I never saw tans like his anymore, even back in California. He had a pleasant enough face—straight nose, tired but lively eyes, even, white teeth when he smiled—which was framed by graying, sandy-brown hair that he'd grown into a short shag that just covered his ears. His body seemed in fairly good shape for a man who looked to be in his fifties. He was tall and probably had once been lanky. He motioned for me to sit down next to him on a low bondage table that took up half the room.

"I was thinking we could start with a role-play where I'm your husband and I've caught you running up our credit card bill. We've agreed previously that anymore reckless shopping sprees would result in an old-fashioned over-the-knee spanking, but you try to talk me out of it because you think it's ridiculous now."

"That sounds fine to me," I nodded.

"Then I was thinking that we could switch, only I don't need you to actually spank me. I just want to pleasure myself while you talk dirty to me about how you would punish me if I were your misbehaving husband," John said.

Suddenly I was alarmed. I had never switched before, and he hadn't mentioned it in the phone call the previous day. If he had, I would have counseled him that I had no experience, and doubted my ability to successfully role-play the punisher instead of the punished. It's something I would have at least wanted to practice, without pay, a couple of times before doing it in a professional session. You wouldn't ask a foot doctor to fix your teeth, and I felt in over my head the same way with his request.

But if I told him, I knew it could mean forfeiting the session and losing out on even more cash for this trip. Not that it was the only consideration, what with having all my expenses paid already, but it wasn't like I'd been raking it in back home before this. Maybe it wouldn't be any more complicated than simply saying things that I knew would turn *me* on from the submissive point of view. *Surely*

*I can play a bitchy woman who wants physical retaliation against an offender. I do it for real almost every day inside my car in L.A. traffic.*

"That's fine, too." I forced what I hoped was a confident smile onto my face.

Through no fault of his own, John and I exchanged some uninspired role-play for the first half hour. *I warned you about what would happen,* he scolded, pulling me gently across his lap. *I can't believe you're serious,* I tried to shout back, but ended up laughing, instead. I was just in too good of a mood to feign outrage at that moment, and was still getting used to kinky improv anyway. After a good warm-up with his hand and an even better light hairbrush spanking, John let me up so we could switch roles.

"You ready?" he asked, after taking off his clothes and stretching out on the bondage table with his legs spread wide. I nodded and climbed up to sit in the large V between his open legs.

"Are there things in particular that push your buttons?" I asked before starting.

"A lot of humiliation. I like the idea of being made to dress up like a girl before being spanked, possibly in front of others."

I realized it would be even easier than I thought, thanks to his helpful details. All I had to do was keep harping on a few key ideas—the embarrassment of being made to cross-dress, his helplessness, being exposed—and I could fish around for any other potential triggers while I talked. I knew from talking to dommes and reading I'd done that a lot of men who liked to cross-dress were not into other men sexually. But some were definitely into the fantasy of a "forced bisexual" encounter. I'd have to see with John.

"You ready? You need any lube or lotion or anything?" I asked, as he began to massage himself into an erection.

"I'm fine, thanks, and yes, I'm ready."

*Please help me get this right for him,* I prayed silently, and began describing my imaginary plans.

"First I'll take you shopping for frilly panties, a pretty pink babydoll dress, black Mary Janes and some new white ankle socks."

I spoke low, hoping it made me sound sexy. "On the way back, we'll stop at a wig store and get you a long blonde head of hair with bangs, just like the little girl in *The Bad Seed*. I'll put it in two braids, and then take you and a lawn chair out into our front yard where all the neighbors can see us."

John moaned and began breathing harder, pulling faster on his erection, his eyes squeezed shut. Most spanking fetishists liked the idea of very "domestic" forms of embarrassment around spanking, not being taken out to an S/M club or another formally kinky environment. They had either been spanked as kids in front of neighbors or friends, or they had wanted to be, and if it wouldn't have freaked out their real neighbors in adulthood, they'd all be out on their lawns right now, too. Running my fingers softly down the insides of John's thighs, I went on.

"If you've been especially bad, I might ask Mr. and Mrs. Jones to come over and help me. I might ask Mrs. Jones to pull you across her knee and lift up the skirt of your dress, and have Mr. Jones pull down those frilly panties so that his wife can spank your bare bottom with the wooden hairbrush I hand her."

"Will you teach me to be a good girl for Mr. Jones?" John gasped at me.

"I might." I smiled, knowing I'd hit pay dirt by mentioning the participation of another guy. "I might have him stand in front of your face while Mrs. Jones punishes you. I might have you unzip his pants—not unbuckle his belt or unbutton the top, but just pull the zipper down, and pull his cock through the open fly. I might have you take your tongue and run it from here"—I used the tip of my index finger to trace a line from the base of his erection to the most sensitive area of the tip—"all the way up to here."

John gasped again and switched hands before returning to his furious stroking. As I went on with my pornographic descriptions of John's apparently ideal block party, I was relieved at how enjoyably effortless this scene had turned out to be.

"What happens if I don't do it right?" he asked, in reference to the blow job he'd be giving Mr. Jones.

"Well," I thought about it for a moment, "in addition to a longer, harder spanking, you might have to learn better technique by watching me, your wife, go down on one of the other neighbors so you can see how it's done."

Another common fantasy of men who liked humiliation was to see their wives with someone else. I waited for John's reaction, to see if I'd gone off track or brought him closer to his end point.

"Really? *Ahhh . . . ahhhhhh.*" He sounded like he was about to come.

*Christ, I'm good at this,* I thought smugly, and looked up expecting to see John finishing himself off in his hand, a serene smile on his face. Instead, what I saw was a limp wrist, a still-hard-but-fading-fast penis, and the slack jaw and closed eyes of a man who was no longer conscious. *Did this man just have a heart attack?* I stared nervously at his chest, and wasn't sure if he was still breathing or not. I did see a quick pulse beating through the thin skin at the bottom of his rib cage. *Can you be alive if your heart's still beating but you're not breathing?* As I hopped off the table so I could come around his side for a closer look, John's chest rose and fell as he abruptly began to snore.

Now it was *my* jaw that went completely slack as I stared at him. I simply could not believe that a person could be so fast asleep, so suddenly and in the midst of such previous, hyper-awake activity. I pressed a hand over my mouth to keep from giggling. Pulling up a chair from another corner of the room, I sat and watched him to make sure he was really sleeping and not in some kind of snoring coma. He looked so vulnerable with his noisy mouth slightly open and everything else so still, I felt like I wished I knew him well enough to do something like kiss him on the forehead. I also felt a little guilty for not nudging him out of his nap, as if I were assisting him in cheating himself out of his paid time with me. But then I thought—*Someone who falls asleep that hard and fast must be really exhausted. Would I want to be woken up if I were having a peaceful doze with a nice person watching over me?*

"Mmph, huh. What's—Are we at my place?" John's eyes fluttered open finally, and he squinted at me in confusion.

"No, baby, we're at the dungeon. You okay?"

"What's going on, what happened?" He sat up on his elbows and looked around.

"You, um, fell asleep for a little bit," I said, trying not to laugh.

"Oh, shit Really? Aw, man, how embarrassing. God! Did I snore? Please tell me I didn't snore." He looked at me with real concern.

"Nah, you didn't snore, you just went out really fast and slept quietly for a few minutes. I didn't know if I should wake you or not—"

"That's okay. I just feel like a big dork. Jesus," he sighed, and rubbed his eyes as he lay back down. "I'm not a weirdo, I swear. I just have sleep apnea, and it makes me have narcoleptic seizures every now and then. Do you know what those are?"

"Yeah. I've known a couple of people who had it. I think one of them got an operation on his nose, and it went away," I offered.

"Actually, I'm scheduled for late this summer, when work should be settled down some," he nodded.

We looked at each other for a couple of seconds, and then I went back over to the bed.

"So, do you want to go back to what we were doing? We have time for you to finish, if you're still in the mood."

"That'd be great!" he grinned, and made room for me on the bondage table before going back to work with his hand.

As strange as it was, it had to be one of the sweetest, easiest afternoons I'd ever had. Even the hot spanking session later that night— with an unexpectedly cute, thirty-something guy who had a thick New York accent and looked Italian enough to get cast in a Martin Scorsese movie—couldn't trump the good feeling that John, and Lissette and Ava before him, had left me with. K had been right: it was a whole different ball game in New York.

It wasn't exactly that I'd been unhappy in L.A. It was more like I felt *extra* capable of happiness in New York City. Like those laundry detergent commercials where the customer doesn't know how dingy her white T-shirt is until they hold up a blindingly clean one next to it, I'd had no idea there was this much excitement, this much desirability to revel in on the east coast. The next day was more of the same—two more spanking sessions with cute, nice guys—and people still calling me for appointments by the time I was walking my luggage back to K's hotel the day after.

"I want to come back next month," I told her excitedly, as we rolled her two large suitcases out of her hotel room.

"I knew you'd love it!" K laughed. "I can give you the woman's number for the sublet if you want it, or you might try Priceline.com as well. I hear they have good deals for hotels. I'm so happy for you that you had such a great time!" she beamed.

"I really did. I don't know how I can ever thank you, or your client, for bringing me here."

"You've already thanked me enough, and my fellow was sorry to miss you, especially after hearing what a wonderful sub you are. I'm sure we'll have a chance to get together on one of your future trips East, now that you're planning on becoming bi-coastal!" she teased.

Although I would have been happy to rehash the details of my trip and to hear about hers, I was secretly relieved when K fell asleep in the cab on the way back to Newark. I wasn't really ready to leave yet, and wanted to take in every last bit of my favorite new place through the windows as we left it behind.

Thinking about the session with John again, I still felt surprised at how well it had gone, all things considered. It had not felt as foreign or difficult as I'd always thought it would for me to be in the opposite role in a session. I didn't necessarily crave more of it just then, but the experience had been more than just pleasant or easy money. Something about it leveled me in a way, too—cut through that part of me that thought it was a nearly unattainable thing to find a satisfying form of sexual dominance in another person. Hell, if I could locate a reasonable facsimile of it in myself, of all places, it couldn't be that hard to find out in the rest of the world, even outside of sessions. If I could so easily be good like that for sleepy John, it seemed a given that someone out there could be good for me, too. Sometimes lately it had even seemed like maybe another woman might be my type. After that first trip to Manhattan, I really felt like the more my world continued to open up through this job, the closer I would come to finding what, and who, I wanted.

# TEN

**"CAN YOU TAKE** this?"

Mistress D attached a pink plastic clothespin to my outer labia and was peering around my legs to see my response.

I nodded, "Yes, Mistress. It's okay."

She put another one on the same side about an inch lower, and then two more on the opposite side. She placed the fifth, and final, clothespin just above the hood of my clitoris. It was a particularly sensitive area, and she smiled when I gasped.

"You're going to take these for me for a little while, aren't you, Marnie?"

D turned so the video camera could capture both the commanding look on her face and my calm nod of agreement in the same shot.

"Good girl."

She went back to fiddling with the clothespins, each of which had a small white string looped through its middle. She tied the ends to the larger ropes around my thighs, so that my lips were pulled open, red and swollen, with the splashes of hot pink looking like so many extended petals on a flower. I knew it looked beautiful because of the mirror straight in front of me.

I had met Mistress D only a couple of hours before, when I came to her studio for this video shoot. I had known *of* her for some time. She was one of the most famous and successful independent dominatrixes in the country. Amazon tall, with long blond hair, a voluptuous body, and as genuinely pretty as any cheerleader I'd gone to school with, she had contacted me a couple of weeks earlier about being a sub in one of her fetish movies. I had been more than flattered, especially when she said she'd heard about me from Mistress K. Working with Mistress D was like receiving the kink equivalent of the Good Housekeeping Seal of Approval.

"Tell me, how does this feel?" she asked, and began tapping the clothespins where they pulled on my tender skin.

I moaned sharply. The pinching intensified when she touched them, but something about the slight movement made everything feel good at the same time.

"It's different, Mistress," I finally answered.

She laughed and stepped away from the table where I lay. "Have you ever felt a vibrator on clamps before, Marnie?" she asked with mock sweetness.

"No, Mistress, I haven't," I said, my voice rising in anxiety.

"Are you afraid it might hurt?" she grinned at me, pulling a large back massager with a phallic attachment on the end out of a nearby drawer.

"Yes, I am," I answered honestly. It wasn't one of the things we had discussed explicitly about the plot. I knew there would be bondage, caning, the clothespins, and some breast flogging, but the vibrator idea was a surprise to me. I calmed down almost immediately, however. I knew she wouldn't be doing anything truly extreme. It was part of our agreement, and she had a reputation for being one of the safest dommes in the scene. As she plugged the device in and brought it back to where she had left me—arms and legs extensively bound and tied together, then hooked onto a suspension cable that lifted my ass slightly off the table—the giant buzzing sound made it hard for me to hear her.

"I asked if you were ready," she said loudly, lightly slapping the back of my thigh.

"I hope so, Mistress," I laughed nervously, and then cried out when she touched the tip of the huge vibrator to the clothespin above my clitoris.

Instead of a sharper pinch, it caused a deep and dull ache, and at the very same time, it provided the intense pleasure that a vibrator normally would when placed in the same spot without clamps. It was the weirdest combination, and I couldn't tell whether I wanted her to turn it off and release me or never, ever stop.

"God, Mistress—*oh, God, please, Mistress,*" I babbled, and pushed my hips toward her.

It was all I could say for the next few minutes as she moved the head over each of the clothespins separately and then pressed it sideways so that it covered them all at the same time. *Please. God. Please, Mistress. Oh, Jesus!,* until I screamed finally, not from an orgasm but from the overload of sensation.

"That's probably enough for now." D feigned mercy for the camera, but it was really time to move on to the next scene.

"Gosh, thank you. That was really neat," I said, after her assistant, Jim, yelled "Cut!" and went out to have a smoke between takes.

"You're welcome," D gazed down at me, having come around to stroke my face after filming stopped. "Thank *you,* for that amazing responsiveness! I knew there was a reason I wanted to work with you," she laughed.

Even having just met her, and even in the context of having to engage in a bit of cheesy posturing for the camera—*Whatever would please you, Mistress; if it amuses you, I will, Mistress*—I still fell fast and hard for D. Lying there, waiting for Jim to come back with a digital camera so he could take promotional stills in this position,

I felt like I would never get tired of staring into her wide, blue eyes. I didn't even mind feeling her hand on my face. The clothespins were simply aching again now that the vibrator was gone, and I was relieved to see Jim come back with the digital camera. Or, relieved as I could be, considering how much I disliked being photographed in the first place.

I hadn't agreed to do the video *just* because of D's professional reputation. I hoped to make a fair amount of money off of it as well. My payment was a master copy of the tape, plus an open-ended agreement for D's production company, i.e., Jim, to provide me with as many copies I wanted at cost. I could sell them to clients and through my Web site at fifty dollars a pop plus postage. Thinking about this new source of possibly steady income made it a little easier to set aside my concerns about the spider veins on my left leg and the tendency of my face to look almost hard on film if I wasn't smiling. The ever-quiet Jim finished up, and I concentrated on my breathing to help get me through the momentary escalation in pain as the clothespins came off. As D released the first one, I yelled in surprise. It was always more intense than I remembered.

"Look at me. I don't want you to lose eye contact with me for the rest of the time when these are coming off, understand?" D ordered, even though the cameras weren't rolling.

I did what she said, staring up at her as she slowly removed the remaining four clamps. Each time, it hurt as bad as the first one, but by the time the last two came off, I could only moan softly at the sharp stabs of pain. As she held my gaze, smiling at my reaction, I felt like I could have worn those things home and slept in them if she'd asked me to.

"*Very* nice, Marnie." D shook her shoulders like she was shaking off a shiver, and waved a manicured hand at her face. "I think I got as much from that as you did," she laughed. "Whew."

As D went about preparing me for the next scene, we got to talking a little about our real lives.

"Where are you from?" she asked, pulling a soft leather sleeve all the way up my arm and fastening its buckles around my wrist and elbow. The sleeve ended in a round mitt on my hand, and once the matching sleeve was on my other arm, I would basically be immobilized from the waist up.

"I'm from here, from Torrance. My parents still live in the house I grew up in, actually."

"Wow. It's not that often that I meet people who are native Angelenos," she said. "So your parents are still married, or is one of them a stepparent?"

"No, they're both my real parents," I shrugged, and slipped my other hand into the bondage sleeve. "You're not from here, yourself?"

"No. I'm from back east originally," D grunted, pulling hard on one of the elbow buckles to get it closed tightly enough to fit me correctly.

"Really? My dad's from Massachusetts. I love the east coast," I said, and it sounded dopey to me as soon as it came out. Like the east coast was similar to a coffee shop down the street or something, and maybe she and my dad's side of the family had run into each other there.

"Yeah, we're from New Hampshire. You've obviously never lived back there," she laughed dryly.

"No, only visited. It's just so green. The first boy I ever French-kissed was in the woods in Massachusetts."

"Turn around now," D instructed, "and put your hands behind you. Lift your wrists up as high as you can."

I obeyed, pulling my wrists toward the middle of my back. She fastened the two sleeves together in four different places, and then walked to the nearby wall and turned a crank to let a suspension hook fall slowly behind me. She stopped when it was about level with my waist.

"So do you still visit?" I asked when she came back over.

She was quiet for a few seconds, and I wondered if I'd hit a sore spot.

"Once in a while I do, Marnie. I'm not super close to my family. I mean I love them, and we certainly get along much better since I've been sober."

"Wow! You're sober? Me too," I smiled.

"Good for you," D smiled back. "You know, it's my birthday this Saturday and I'm having some people over. You should come. My parents will even be there. You guys can bond over your love of the northeast," she joked.

Pushing my upper back gently so that I was tilted forward just a few inches more, she slipped the suspension hook through one of the rings at my now-conjoined elbows. She then went back to pull the hook up a little higher so that I would be firmly held in place, ass fully exposed for flogging for the scene we were about to shoot. It was a surprisingly comfortable position, and I relaxed into it, shutting my eyes so I could enjoy the fantasy of being introduced to her parents as her girlfriend some day, instead of merely a friend from work.

"Aw, look at you, all dressed up!" D said, grabbing me in a quick hug and ushering me into the foyer of her two-story house on a quiet street in Hollywood.

I had worn a skirt, with a soft cotton blouse that showed some cleavage but still managed to look almost conservative. I wasn't sure what were the right clothes to wear to a dominatrix's birthday party. D had said it wasn't a play party, and of course her parents would be there. I'd tried to look attractive without putting on anything that might have drawn stares from her neighbors as I came up the front walk.

"This is my friend, Lisa. Lisa, can you show Marnie where she can put her purse? And you already know Jim."

D nodded into a small room off to the left where Jim waved and went back to watching a video he was running on the large-screen television.

"Nice to meet you," I said, and shook Lisa's hand.

She was a petite brunette who looked to be in her late twenties. She motioned for me to follow her deeper into the house. Lisa was wearing a latex French maid's outfit, and used the toy duster in her hand to playfully brush a couple of the people we passed as she led me to a back bedroom.

"You can leave your stuff in here, and the bathroom's back there if you'd be more comfortable changing in it—" She looked confused as she noticed all I had on me was my purse.

"Um, I'm not actually—I didn't bring anything to change into," I said, blushing.

Virtually all of the partygoers we'd passed were dressed in kinky gear. D herself had been wearing a full length, black catsuit with a tightly cinched black corset and thigh-high leather boots. But it hadn't registered on me at first: after all, I was used to seeing her in full regalia.

"Oh." Lisa seemed at a loss for words. "Well—that's okay. You look fine how you are, Marnie," she recovered quickly.

I had thought so, too, initially. Now I wanted to run into the bathroom, tear off the clear plastic shower curtain, and cut it into hot pants and a halter top. *D must have really liberal parents,* I thought as I set my purse on a dresser near the doorway before following Lisa back out to the party.

"Marnie, this is my father, Joe, and this is my stepmother, Brenda."

D had found me hovering awkwardly near the small buffet table in the kitchen. I hadn't seen anyone else I knew at the party, and I felt a little too self-conscious to approach the small groups of well-dressed perverts milling around. I'd been relieved when she'd asked me to come meet her folks. They were sitting stiffly at a small card table in the main living room toward the back of the house.

"Hello," I smiled politely as we all shook hands.

Joe looked to be in his late sixties, a tall, slim man with a ring of short gray hair around a mostly bald head. Brenda looked about ten years younger, with light brown hair in a neat bob, and sparkling eyes under a thick pair of bifocals with a horn-rimmed frame. They were the only people I'd seen so far who looked as square and out-of-place as I felt.

"Is this seat taken?" I pointed to an empty chair next to Brenda.

"No, please," she gestured for me to join them.

"Marnie has family back east," D offered helpfully. "*Oo,* I think I hear Max at the front door! I'll be back."

She gave a quick grin and disappeared into the crowd of her friends. The three of us looked at each other, looked at our hands, scanned the crowd, looked back at each other. *We are so uncomfortable here. Thank God, I found my people.*

"So D told me you guys are from New Hampshire?" I finally said.

"Yes, Shannon—we know her as Shannon," D's dad laughed nervously, "spent most of her childhood with us, then moved out here when she was just eighteen."

"And do you like visiting out here, or you like it back home better? If that's not too personal—"

"Oh no," Brenda smiled warmly, "it's not too personal. It's fun to visit L.A., but we're definitely more at home back at, you know, home," she laughed. "What about you, Marnie? You're from the east coast originally?"

"I wish," I laughed softly, oddly flattered by the idea that I might pass for someone who was. "I grew up out here. My dad's from Massachusetts, a little ways north of Boston. My favorite cousins live in Woburn, and I'm hoping to visit them in the next couple of months," I said, thinking I might take a train to Boston for a night or so the next time I went to New York.

"Oh, that's great," Joe said, nodding.

"Well, I shouldn't say they're my *favorite* cousins. I love all my cousins. The ones near Boston are just more like friends, you know, close to my age. We have a good time."

"That's nice that you're so close to your family." Brenda reached over and patted my hand. "Not that it's anyone's fault, but I know a lot of Shannon's *other* friends," she raised her eyebrows and whispered conspiratorially, "seem to come from pretty hard backgrounds. Many of them don't have any contact with their families at all."

"I know. It's a sad thing," I said, thinking about how not-nice and not-close my relationship had been with my immediate family before I'd gotten sober. "I'm pretty lucky."

"So, if you don't mind me asking, Marnie," Joe leaned in and spoke quietly, "how did you meet Shannon? I didn't know she had many friends outside of the—uh—*scene* she's into."

"Oh." For some reason I had thought that D would have told them how we knew each other. "Well, I'm actually—sort of—from that scene, too, I guess you could say," I finished hesitantly.

Joe's and Brenda's eyebrows flew up simultaneously.

"But you're so—normal," Joe whispered. "I don't mean to say that there's anything bad about it," he added quickly, holding up his hands in a hey-no-judgment-here gesture.

I laughed, relieved that they wanted to find a polite way to address it just like I did.

"In fairness, I will say that I've met some really decent people in this business and in the broader," I cleared my throat nervously, "kink scene in general. But I do know what you mean. I probably look more like a librarian than someone who makes a living this way."

"So do your parents know?" Brenda obviously still couldn't believe it.

"Yeah, they know. Most of the people in my life know, except my little-old-lady Catholic aunts back in Massachusetts," I said.

"They weren't upset when you told them?" Joe asked. "I mean, we never got *angry* at Shannon or threatened to disown her or anything, but it definitely took some getting used to."

"I'm still not that used to it." Brenda shook her head.

"They didn't act upset, at least to my face. I guess I should tell you I had a pretty serious drug problem when I was a little younger," I said, watching their eyes widen in shock a second time. "I think after seeing me struggle to get through that, they just figured as long as I was alive and sober, they weren't gonna worry too much about anything else. I mean, I'm sure they'll be glad when I'm not doing this anymore, but they don't give me a hard time about it."

It was a little strange to go from feeling so relaxed with them to knowing they now found me hard to understand. Sometimes I felt like I was both too geeky for the freaks and too freaky for the squares. Joe and Brenda nodded politely, but I think we were all relieved when D came to get me a few minutes later.

"I have to steal Marnie away from you now. I need to ask her something in *private.*" D gave the last word an exaggerated sensuality and winked at me.

"It was really nice meeting you both," I said, and meant it, as I got up from the table.

"Yes, you too," Brenda said, grasping my hand warmly in hers.

"Take care of yourself, Marnie. Be careful," Joe said with a fatherly tone.

I turned to follow D into her quiet office upstairs.

"I *love* your parents," I sighed, still touched by how kind they'd been to me. "Thanks for inviting me."

"Thank *you,*" D purred. "I like to surround myself with little pleasures, even during work. E*specially* during work," she giggled, raising her eyebrows at me.

Now that we were alone together, I was unable to stop myself from hoping that it might have something to do with the mutual chemistry she'd clearly felt during our shoot those few days earlier.

"Thanks for coming," D smiled. She stared at me silently for a moment, and finally spoke again. "I really enjoyed playing with you the other day, Marnie. You have a great deal to offer as a submissive, and it was truly a pleasure being on the receiving end of some of it."

"Gosh, thank you," I said, surprised at her directness. I reminded myself that after all, she was a domme.

"You have a good head on your shoulders," she went on. "You're sincere and intelligent, and I have to tell you I really like that you're sober. I've been thinking about you a lot in the last few days."

"I've been thinking about you, too," I ventured. "It was kind of hard not to."

"Good." D tilted her head and smiled wide. "I'm so glad to hear that. Because I really want to have a closer relationship with you. I'd like to bring you in as one of the family, so to speak."

It wasn't exactly as thrilling for me as if she'd asked me to go steady. I had always thought that being part of a leather family would grate on me, especially if I was identified as a sub in the group. From what I'd heard, leather families were sort of the kinky lifestylers' version of Mormon polygamy, complete with formal hierarchies and the general subordination of all members to a single head of the family. Granted, there wasn't much concern for sinning in leather families, but still I hadn't ever imagined that set-up as my style. Looking into D's eyes as she leaned toward me, her lips slightly parted—was she about to say something, or was she about to kiss me?—I re-evaluated my previous opinion in a flash. I already sensed that D viewed me with more respect than I might have received in any male-run group, and I didn't actually know *that* much about what went on in leather families. Maybe I was being too quick to judge.

"My current assistant is leaving, you see, moving to San Francisco at the end of the month. It's a part-time position, only six hours a day, and I'm pretty flexible about which six. You'd usually have weekends off, and I could pay you fifteen dollars an hour, plus bonuses. Any time you're responsible for booking the space for outside use—Hollywood films, private parties—you get forty percent of the rental fee. You could still do your own sessions as well, and never have to pay a rental fee for that either."

She sat back in her chair, seemingly satisfied that she'd sold this job as a great opportunity for me. I was literally struck dumb. She wanted me to be her *secretary?* I thought she had contacted me in the first place because of my growing success as an independent pro sub. Where did she think I'd find thirty hours a week to be her right arm? Wait, *fuck* that. Where did she get the idea that I would even *want* to be her busy little sidekick, even if I *did* have the time? Since when had I indicated a willingness to be absorbed into someone else's demanding life instead of continuing to work to build up my own? And then the final indignity hit me. I knew there was no way in hell she would ever have floated such an idea past an independent pro domme. No matter what I thought I had felt with D, our roles were fixed as far as she was concerned. People who got turned on by certain things were there to serve, and people who got turned on by other certain things were there to *be* served. I was one, she was the other. No amount of business sense, smarts, or sobriety in common would change that in D's mind. I took a deep breath, sat up straight, and looked her in the eye.

"Thanks for the offer, but I'm actually happy doing what I'm doing right now," I said evenly.

She looked momentarily flustered. "Well, of course you could still do what you're doing. I thought I made that clear?"

"D, I *left* a job as a secretary to get into this work in the first place. It's just not what I'm looking for. But thanks," I said again, standing up to leave.

"Well."

From the look on her face, it must have been quite a while since anyone she viewed as submissive had told her anything but *Yes, Mistress*. She didn't get up, and I didn't look back. I wasn't even that mad by the time I got out to my car. I'm sure in her mind she was conferring a great honor on me when she offered to let me work for her. By the time I was home, I was laughing about it. *Can you imagine if she had wanted to date you? Talk about high maintenance—the girl can't even answer her own phones.* So much for my latest daydream. Apparently it wasn't the X and Y chromosomes, after all, that made a difference in who might be a good match for me and who wouldn't.

## ELEVEN

**BUSINESS PICKED UP** a little in Los Angeles after I made the video with D. Being mentioned on her Web site as she promoted the new flick seemed to be what was helping. And, in addition to the money and physical satisfaction of being busier, I loved that I got to see Catherine more. She wasn't the type—and didn't have the free time—to just hang around chatting aimlessly; she was, however, always happy to answer my questions about anything that came up. I made sure to have a lot of them.

"Are there any women who have private spaces like yours in New York?" I was waiting for a client to arrive at the dungeon, watching her reorganize the large closet in her office that was filled with fetish clothes.

"Yeah. One of my best friends has her own place. That's where I do my sessions whenever I'm back there."

Catherine pulled a dark violet, floor-length slip dress off a hanger and put it in a bag marked for dry cleaning. I had really liked

Lissette, and the space she shared with Ava was lovely, but I felt more attracted to the idea of renting from other independents. I felt like they were my people now, and the idea of being even more in Catherine's circle, in particular, by renting from her best friend back east, was too tempting to pass up.

"Do you think she might let me use her place too when I'm in New York again?"

"Oh yeah, she'd totally rent to you. You guys would love each other," Catherine smiled.

The sight of that smile made me feel a little like swooning. Catherine almost never smiled. It wasn't like she came across as depressed or cranky; she just wasn't given to polite and empty gestures of approval. She could even utter her dry laugh without changing her facial expression whatsoever. I liked the effect her smile rationing had. When her mouth spread into a grin that changed her whole face from pretty to breathtaking, it felt like seeing all the cherries line up on a slot machine. It'd be less exciting if it happened every time you slipped a quarter in.

"I'll be in session when you get out today, but I'll tape a note to your bag with my friend's phone number on it. She goes by Nurse Wolf professionally, but you can call her 'W'. I'll ring her up right now so she knows to expect you."

I was still dazzled by how nice most of these independent pro dommes were. I realized, of course, that it wasn't necessarily just out of the kindness of their hearts; clearly anyone who had a private dungeon stood to gain a fair amount of rent money by making me happy at her place. Even so, from Lissette's flirting to K's taking me to New York to Catherine's offer to make introductions, none of these women seemed to be phony or self-serving. All any of them really had to do was just provide a safe, nice place to work and not be an asshole. Anything else was beyond the call of duty.

I tried not to get carried away with the idea of how wonderful it was now that I was working on my own. I figured the bottom could fall out at any time, like it had at the Dominion, or with K. Yet I remained mostly convinced that I was being cosmically rewarded for taking a chance instead of playing it safe and going back to some dull, straight job.

"Hey sweetie!" W threw open the heavy front door and grabbed me in a tight hug. "So good to meet you, finally!"

"You too," I laughed as she let me go.

I had flown into JFK the night before, and my first two sessions of the trip were doubles with W.

"If you want, you can change in my office." She pointed to a door behind us. "Or in the bathroom, which is this way."

She led me down a long hallway to a small foyer that branched into a kitchen, a dimly-lit dungeon room, and the bright, white bathroom. W was already dressed for our first session when she let me in, decked out in a classic black lingerie set complete with garter belt and stockings. She had the lean, tan, muscular upper body of a surfer girl, and watching her strut down the hallway in front of me felt like being at my own private Victoria's Secret fashion show. I would have liked W even if she hadn't been as beautiful as she was, but that didn't enable me to ignore the superficial stuff. I don't even know how to say this in an inoffensive way, but her small waist flared into the roundest, most amazing ass I had ever seen on a white woman, never mind a blonde. There was nothing typically blond about her, in fact, from the rear view to her big brown eyes and exotically-chiseled face. Her shoulder-length hair definitely looked like her natural color, though.

"This will be fine," I said, and set my bag on the clean tiles of the bathroom floor. I had brought a variation on the outfit W wore—stockings, heels, and garter belt, as the first client wanted me to be essentially naked. While I changed, W filled me in on what we'd be doing.

"You're basically just going to be dealing with me. He wants us to pretend like he's not even there. He's a big punishment guy. He wants to see a female sub endure some pretty intense corporal for the first part of the session, and then you'll leave and I'll switch to punishing him."

I felt nervous when she first explained it to me. I hadn't known that it was going to be a heavier session, and I hadn't decided before then what kind of money I wanted for more intense scenes. Although it had never come up for me when I'd been working at the Dominion, I'd heard that subs were allowed to require an extra hundred dollars as a marking fee if they did heavy sessions there. Surely I could get more as an independent than the two hundred and fifty per hour I normally charged. I didn't want to sound greedy, but I had to talk to W about it.

"I generally accept a higher donation for heavy sessions," I told her, as if it were something I already had a lot of experience with. "What's the best way to, you know, deal with the money stuff with this guy?"

"Oh, you don't need to worry about that. He's unusually generous anyway. We never talk about money. He just hands me a wad of bills at the end, and it's always way more than my normal fee. It'll be the same for you," she said.

I wasn't sure what to say to that. My feeling about W came from the fact that I'd trusted her pretty instantly when we'd first talked on the phone. She seemed to enjoy my sense of humor, and she talked to me like there was no such thing as one of us being a dominant and one a submissive, in sessions or anywhere else. Still, we were technically strangers, and the whole thing felt somewhat unnatural to me. I was used to handling my money a certain way. And I'd never even heard of letting a client pay whatever he wanted after the session was over, let alone considered such a thing myself. The buzzer rang before I could sort out what I wanted to say, and as W left to let the client in, I finished changing. She returned a few minutes later to get me, and I followed her down the hall with as open a mind as I could muster.

"Come over here and get across my lap," she ordered, sitting with her legs stretched in front of her on the large Persian rug in the middle of the room.

There was a gurney-sized bondage table in one corner and a regular-sized couch against the nearest wall, close to the door. The client who sat on it and watched us was in full Orthodox Jewish regalia. W later told me he wasn't one, but I forever after thought of him as *The Rabbi*.

"Why did I get here today to find unwashed dishes in the kitchen?" W demanded, holding me around the waist as I lay across her knees, my arms and legs on the floor on either side of her.

"Um, I guess I forgot to do them before I left last night?" I improvised. It caught me a little off guard that we were doing a role-play, but it was easy enough to slip into.

"You *guess?*"

W brought a slender hand down on my ass with a quick snap. It stung, but I could tell it was intentionally a warm-up slap, meant to look worse than it was so we could build up to a more intense level. It was easier on a person's body than starting heavy to begin with.

"No, I mean yes, I flat-out forgot to do them last night. I'm sorry."

I laughed when I said it, partly out of nervousness—I still didn't know exactly where this was going—and partly because I was just happy.

I considered myself genetically half-Catholic, having grown up in an atheist household, but with a father who had been devout until he was in college. I had always been fascinated with the stories my cousins on that side of the family would tell me about parochial school, where corporal punishment was allowed. God, how many times I had fantasized in my life about being in just this position, with some religious authority presiding over a spanking I probably didn't even deserve. And The Rabbi was going to pay me for it? How could I not have laughed?

"You're obviously *not* sorry, but you will be," W warned, and began spanking me at a continuous, methodical pace.

She had a surprisingly hard hand. It felt more like being spanked by a lumberjack than by this slim blond goddess. She stopped after a few minutes, just as I was starting to get used to it.

"I want you to pick out two different canes from the ones on those hooks over there."

She helped me up and pointed toward the far wall. They hung there from black iron hooks, in different sizes and shapes. Not yet having much experience with these things, I wasn't sure which ones to grab. There was a thin one much like the cane Marcus had used on me that had felt so good, so I picked it up and held it under one arm while I considered the others.

"I don't have all day, and you're making it worse the longer you stall!" W called out to me.

I hurriedly picked the closest one to me, one similar to the other I held but twice as thick in diameter. I presented them to W and stood with my hands behind my back, hoping I was making a good impression on The Rabbi.

"Get on your knees in front of the couch, and lean over with your elbows on the cushion so that your bottom is presented to me nicely."

I knelt down next to The Rabbi's legs and positioned myself a few inches away from him. Because he was a somewhat sizable man, there wasn't much room to leave between us and still be on the same couch. I figured W would tell me if I was too close to him, so I put my head down on the couch and waited.

"You're going to take six hard strokes with each of these, and you're not going to move out of position or make an unseemly amount of noise while you're taking your punishment. Is that understood?"

"Yes, Mistress," I said, no longer as lighthearted as I'd felt moments before.

The sound of what she was planning to do excited me, but after getting a taste of that Popeye arm of hers with just the hand-spanking, I guessed the caning she was about to give me might hurt a great deal. I started taking slow, deep breaths.

"We'll try the thick one first. Raise your ass up a little more for me—good. Ready?"

"I think so, Mistress," I said, and felt my body tense.

A second later, the thick cane drove a searing line of pain into my skin. I moaned, and felt something touch my hands. I'd pressed my face into the cushions to muffle myself in case the caning made me yell, and when I looked up I saw The Rabbi's right hand covering both of mine. I hadn't realized I was holding mine together like I was praying, and I was surprised by the tenderness of his gesture. His hand was pale, with hair down to his knuckles, and deep wrinkles visible up to his wrist where his arm disappeared into a long, dark sleeve. Up to that point I had simply imagined him as a cold, almost academic observer.

The second stroke hurt as much if not more than the first, and that time I did scream into the cushions. The Rabbi took his hand from mine and placed it on the back of my head, slowly running his palm over my hair as I caught my breath before the caning continued. It was unexpectedly comforting, but I felt like I needed something more to help me through.

"Mistress, may I please touch myself while you're caning me?"

It wasn't necessarily that I was so turned on by it all, but I had learned, back in my days with T, that rubbing my clitoris could act as a sort of mild painkiller during certain torments. It wouldn't have worked for getting a filling at the dentist's office, but it had helped me not only endure but even enjoy some things that might otherwise have been pretty difficult. When W gave me the go-ahead, I slowly pulled my right hand out of The Rabbi's grasp and slipped it between my legs.

As W resumed caning me, the work of my right hand caused me to go from stiff anticipation of each stroke to nearly drooling immersion in the different sensations that were overwhelming my body. One second I would be gasping from the pain of the latest swing of the cane, nearly weeping from the surprise and severity of it, and the next I would be craving more of that same ache, as it seemed to accentuate what I was feeling between my legs. By the time W was done caning me, what had started as a way to help myself through the ordeal had turned into the single focus of my attention.

"Mistress, would it be okay for me to make myself come, now?" I asked, hoping such a self-serving request wouldn't put a damper on The Rabbi's fantasy hour.

"Absolutely," W purred at me, and came to sit near me by the couch.

It was awkward to try and come in this position, leaning forward on my knees, but The Rabbi's silent encouragement coupled with the stimulation of what W had just done pushed my buttons in a way that had me breathless before I knew what hit me. With W stroking my hair on one side and The Rabbi clutching my left hand on the other, I quickly came not once, but three times before my entire body was so fatigued I had to lie down in front of the couch.

"That's my girl," W grinned down at me.

"Jesus," I exhaled. "Thank you, Mistress."

"Thank *you,* that was amazing," she laughed.

It wasn't the first time I'd had an orgasm in session. I had soon discovered at Catherine's that there were plenty of clients who got aroused by watching me come. Frankly it had surprised me that a client would spend a good chunk of his paid time watching and waiting for me to climax, since it hadn't usually been as quick there as with W and The Rabbi. As liberal as my views were about what sexual submission could look like, the one thing that hadn't previously occurred to me was that it could look like a career in compulsive masturbation. Which isn't to say that I got to come in session every time I felt like it, or that I even felt like it all the time; sometimes the exchanges left my body in a state of arousal and subsequent satisfaction that seemed to bypass the concept of orgasm altogether. Still, in its own way it was a confidence-builder for me. I seemed to have a real talent for churning out orgasms in front of an audience. When things sometimes got slow in sessions, it was my ace in the hole, as far as showmanship went.

As I was gathering myself to leave, The Rabbi surprised me by speaking for the first time.

"Thank you," he said softly.

I looked up to see him smiling warmly at me, and I thanked him, too, before slipping out the door.

I changed back into my street clothes and waited in the office while W finished the session. We were set to do our second appointment together about an hour after The Rabbi's time was up so there was no point in leaving and coming back. Still a little jet-lagged, I started to drift off on the comfortable love seat next to her desk, and woke up to the sound of the front door closing.

"This is for you," W said moments later, handing me a thick wad of bills. "That was great. Are you okay? I wasn't too hard on you?"

I shook my head. "God, no. It was awesome!"

I looked at the money in my hands, a little self-conscious about caring how much was there, but curious nonetheless. What I had first taken to be several twenties turned out to be twelve one-hundred-dollar bills.

"Whoa—are you sure this is for me and not *us?*"

"Yeah. It's all yours. He gave me mine at the end," W laughed. "He must have really liked you. This is the most money he's ever paid anyone I brought him, and the most he's paid me as well!"

I couldn't believe it. I had been in there barely over thirty minutes, and he had paid me twelve hundred dollars for it. Despite the Orthodox Jewish thing, he was Santa Claus as far as I was concerned.

An hour later, W prepped me for our second session.

"I've been seeing him for years now, and it's taken this long for us to figure out even a little of what he likes," she whispered as she rifled through an open drawer in her dressing closet. The client, Al, was in the next room waiting for us to get dressed. "Here, put these on." She held out an unopened package of beige pantyhose. "And then, let's see—okay, you can wear my cowboy boots. They're over there by the door."

I took the panty hose and started getting undressed. "Should I wear a bra and panties too, or just a bra if he likes the pantyhose by themselves?"

"No, no, just the hose and the boots. No bra, nothing else." W began pulling on a pair of similar stockings.

"Wow," I said, wondering how in the world this man could find such a get-up sexy on me.

Or on anyone, really. W's cowboy boots were too big for me, and I had to scrunch my toes to sort of hold on to the soles so my feet wouldn't slide out. I gingerly practiced walking around the closet, which was actually a small room that had been converted. Satisfied that I could at least move around without stumbling, I joined W in front of the full-length mirror that hung on the back of the door. She had on a leather thong and leather bra with her panty hose and another pair of boots. Like most pro dommes, she didn't even get topless in session, let alone fully naked.

"You look great." She smiled at my reflection. "Ready?"

Al was waiting for us, completely nude on a leather bench, when W ushered me through the door and introduced us. He had a cute, New-York-Irish-guy face, with light brown hair and a stocky build. He also had the biggest cock I'd ever seen in real life.

"Hi." He held up a hand to me and grinned.

"Look what I brought you. Isn't she adorable?" W stood next to me and stroked my hair. "Turn around, let him see the whole beautiful package."

I clomped around to face away from Al as daintily as I could, and W put a hand on my arm to bring me back full circle. It looked convincingly mistressy to Al, I imagined, but I knew from the light pressure of her fingers and the look in her eyes that she was just trying to help me keep my balance, bless her heart.

"So." W touched Al and me lightly as she moved from one of us to the other and back again. "What shall we do with Marnie today, Al?"

He shrugged and grinned, true to W's description of a man who had no clue. She took him by the hand anyway and pulled him close to me, then placed his same hand on my breast. Al gave a tentative squeeze, and then brought his other hand up to my body.

"She has soft skin, Mistress," he murmured to W.

"Mm, yes, she does."

As Al caressed my front and W caressed his back, I hoped my downward gaze made me look thoughtfully submissive rather than like a person with a staring problem. I could not take my eyes off of Al's huge—even at half-mast—cock. The thought of what it must feel like to have something that size inside of me was even more distracting than the mere sight of it.

I tended to associate the right kind of pain during sex with increased pleasure, not because of the whole S/M thing, but because of how I had lost my virginity. What had happened was this: after settling on a good candidate when I was twenty, I drank three wine coolers in preparation, stretched out on his bed, and could not for the life of me take him in. It literally felt like he was pushing on something that didn't have an opening, no matter how much lubrication and finger action he used ahead of time. Finally, after a solid two weeks of repeated attempts, I suggested we try it with me on top. Ignore my *ows,* I told him, and don't stop unless I say *stop.* It never technically quit hurting even once he was inside, but it felt so good, too, that it was all I wanted to do for the next six months straight. From that perspective, looking at Al's potential made me feel like I thought a rock climber would looking at Mt. Everest.

"Why don't we tie Marnie to the table?" W suggested, interrupting my not-quite nostalgic reverie.

"Sounds great!" He put a hand on my arm to lead me there.

"May I take my boots off so I can climb up more easily?" I asked, sure that I would otherwise fall off the stool W had brought over to help me up.

"Yes, you may, and then just get in whatever position is most comfortable for you."

After I stretched out flat on my back, W put cuffs on my wrists, while Al put them on my ankles, and then W used short pieces of rope to tie each cuff to the eyehooks on the sides of the table. She worked slowly, and I tried to help kill time by making suggestions, like adjusting one of the cuffs on my feet.

"Now—what shall we do with helpless, beautiful Marnie?" W put a finger up to her mouth thoughtfully.

The gesture made me laugh, and then W and Al laughed too.

"How about you, Marnie? Why don't we make it your job to come up with something?" W teased.

"Um, okay. Can I ask what my choices are?"

"Let's say whatever you want—those are the choices." W ran her hand lightly over my stomach.

I tried to look thoughtful for the next minute or so, even though my head kept repeating the same thing over and over—*sex with Al sex with Al sex with Al.* I was afraid to say it out loud because I didn't think it was an option. The world of independent kinksters might not be as rigid as the Dominion, but there's a big difference between not caring whether I got naked and touched myself versus being okay with flat-out prostitution. *Plus,* I thought, *wouldn't Al himself have gone to see a regular escort if regular sex was what he was after?*

"You look confused," W prompted. Her voice was kind and patient.

"I feel like the one thing that's coming to mind is—I don't know—inappropriate or something," I finally blurted.

"Well, *now* you definitely have to tell us," she laughed.

Al waited expectantly by the foot of the bondage bed.

"It's not like—" I began, but W cut me off.

"No disclaimers. In a perfect world where you could do whatever you wanted right now, what would it be?"

I looked at Al's cute face and avoided dropping my gaze to below his waist. I turned my eyes back to W and sighed nervously.

"I'm just curious what it would feel like to have someone as big as Al inside me," I said in a rush.

"Great!" W answered immediately, her tone no different than if I had just suggested a game of Parcheesi. "Hop on up, Al, and I'll get the condoms."

As the still-silent Al climbed onto the table and positioned himself between my legs, W returned with a couple of Trojans and a tube of K-Y. I wondered how he really felt about it. I know it's not easy for guys to turn down sex, even if they really want to. I'm not saying I could think of any reason why he wouldn't want to do it with me, just that I didn't like the idea of how quickly he was in a position where he might have felt pressured into it. As he hovered over me and tore open one of the condoms, I caught his eye.

"We don't have to do this if you don't want to," I whispered. "I didn't mean to put you on the spot."

"Are you kidding?" Al chuckled.

As I lay there, looking at W while she watched us, I felt like I could not have loved two people more even after knowing them for years, never mind the short time it had actually been. Al felt even better than I would have imagined, and there was something about having W there—sometimes standing back and sometimes stroking Al's smooth back or my hair—that made me feel even more penetrated by her than by him.

"You're like Mr. Rourke," I said to her dreamily, thinking of the eighties television show *Fantasy Island*, "only much, much cuter, no hard feelings to Ricardo Montalban."

W threw back her head and laughed, and I realized how dopey I probably sounded. I didn't ask about my own orgasm in this session, partly because I was still worn out from the previous three and partly because I don't really need or even like to come during intercourse. For me, orgasms and the friction of fucking are two distinct and equally enjoyable pleasures. I know it's not that way for a lot of women, but to me it's like loving two different foods. I never get tired of the taste of bacon or Haagen Daaz chocolate ice cream, but I don't miss one when I'm having the other.

And Al was great at fucking. Not to give less-endowed guys a complex, because if I were hot for someone they could have an acorn down there for all I care, but for someone who *did* have a cock, he was skilled at using it. He lasted the perfect amount of time, around ten minutes I guessed, and he teased me mercilessly by going slow and almost stopping for the first several minutes, then moving fast and hard inside me until he finished with a loud moan and collapsed on top of me. Fortunately he was considerate enough to lift himself back onto his elbows after only a couple of seconds, allowing my lungs to inflate fully again.

"That was fantastic!" W sounded proud of all three of us.

Al pulled his clothes on while W untied me, but I stayed where I was, totally spent even though I hadn't actually moved a muscle.

Al came to kiss me on the cheek before heading to the front door with W.

"Hope to see you again," he said.

I hoped so, too, although I felt like I would need to tell him that I wasn't really an escort and couldn't guarantee I'd want to fuck again. We would have to see how it went. I didn't want to automatically feel like that was my job, now. *But you did just have sex with someone who gave you money, so what makes you "not an escort?"* I wondered if the fact that I had initiated it instead of negotiated for it made any difference. One of the first things I said to people when I told them what I did for a living was *I don't have actual sex with the clients or anything,* and it always seemed to set people at ease after the initial shock. Most everyone in my life already knew what I did, and I doubted any of them would want me to issue an addendum on the subject. But what about any new friends I made, or if, at some point, I did end up wanting to date again? I didn't want to lie, either.

*But why should I have to,* I suddenly wondered? I didn't even agree with the stigma attached to prostitutes, whether they walked the streets or worked for Heidi Fleiss. I didn't particularly like the conditions that led to and surrounded prostitution on a large scale, but I knew the people who made a living that way weren't a different species of human. Why was it so important to differentiate myself from them in the first place?

I was watchful for any sign that having sex in a session had fundamentally changed me in some way. I didn't want to wake up in some kind of shame spiral, finding out too late that I had violated an unexpected psychological or emotional boundary I hadn't been aware of before. In fact, it never happened. I didn't know whether this meant that what I did with Al couldn't be so easily catalogued, or whether I was perhaps already as messed up as I was ever going to get, and maybe that carried a weird sort of untouchability of its own. All I knew for sure at the end of that trip was that New York was still magic for me.

## TWELVE

**"HI, MARNIE. LISTEN,** it's Steve. I wanted to ask you out on a date for Saturday while you're here; a professional date. There's a party that I'd like to pay you to attend with me. Call me when you get in."

The voice mail had beeped on my phone as soon as I landed at JFK, for my third working visit. I'd met Steve on the last trip. He had called to ask me to join him and his regular mistress for a session in which they would both dominate me. He said he was normally submissive, and he sounded nice. W had vouched for his mistress, C, so I figured I would be in good hands even if it was Steve's first time switching.

It turned out that I was in great hands. C had been dreamy—sexy as hell, throaty voice I could listen to all day, and a perfect mixture of reassuring kindness and good-humored cruelty. Steve, however, had been another matter altogether.

"He's a really great guy. He just gets a little excited sometimes," C told me as we changed together before the session. "He has his special leather pants and everything, and wants to be addressed as Master Steve today," she rolled her eyes. but it was obvious that she found Steve cute above and beyond his slight goofiness.

Cute turned into cause for ending things early when Steve's enthusiasm propelled him to reach back and grab C awkwardly by her hips, as she entered him from behind with a strap-on. A little more than halfway into our session, Steve had asked to be penetrated. But where C had expected the sweet submissive she knew and liked, Steve had instead given her a virtual mechanical bull ride, bucking so hard he lifted her off the ground. It seemed like the indignity of it was made even worse for C by the fact that I was there to witness it. I tried to reassure her that none of his oafishness had rubbed off on her in my eyes, but she was furious with him. He sent me an e-mail a few days later, begging me to explain what he'd done wrong, and how he could get back into C's good graces. The poor bastard truly hadn't understood why she'd refused to speak to him after the session. I had never met anyone before who was both that earnest and that much of a buffoon at the same time, and it had made me like Steve more than a little. We had not spoken since he'd written to thank me for helping straighten things out with C. I returned his call from the cab on the way to my hotel.

"So what kind of party are we talking about?"

"A swingers' party."

I cleared my throat. "What . . . would we do at a . . . swingers' party?"

I'd never been to one, and it sounded like a possible adventure. At the same time, I didn't know whether he meant to imply that he would be swinging me around or what.

"*You* don't have to do anything; I just need someone to go with me—single men can't get in alone."

"So you plan to do whatever it is you want to do, and I'm just there to get you in the door? We're not talking about me, you know, having sex or anything?"

"Right."

"What time Saturday night?"

"Uh, it depends on when I can sneak out of my house. The party's starting pretty late. I'll probably pick you up around eleven-thirty or so."

"You've gotta sneak out? So that means there's a chance this might not happen at all, then?" I had grave doubts about Steve's ability to commit an act of stealth with any success whatsoever.

"It'll happen," Steve said, and, to his credit, he didn't even sound defensive. "I just have to wait for my wife to fall asleep. I'll tell you what, though. I'll bring you an hour's worth of your fee for a deposit. That way if anything goes wrong, you'll at least not have wasted your time waiting around, and you can keep the money no matter what."

It sounded rather ideal by that point. I'd make some kind of money regardless, and if I actually worked that night it would be the easiest job I'd ever had, watching people mess around with each other.

I agreed to meet Steve the next day at a coffee shop next door to W's place after a session. When I first saw his tall frame, brown hair, and babyish face, I smiled and raised my hand. He looked away as if he hadn't recognized me. The whole front of the coffee place was open like a sidewalk café, with a few tables in a row between the street and where I sat just inside. As I watched, puzzled, Steve began to walk back and forth in front of the row of tables with his back stiff and his eyes straight ahead. He looked like one of those fake ducks that moves from one side of a shooting gallery to the other. Suddenly he turned sideways and scooted through two tables to make his way over to me. Plopping down next to me, he took a wad of cash from his pants pocket and jabbed it in my direction. He would not put it directly in my hand.

"What—am I supposed to let you set it down before I pick it up?"

I said it gently, but felt like I was getting ready to smack him. Not in a mean way—more like you would cuff a vending machine that was malfunctioning. Abruptly, he shoved the folded bills into my front jeans pocket without saying a word. I gave him a polite smile and waited.

"So I'll call you around eleven-thirty or twelve on Saturday night, once my wife's asleep."

"Have you ever snuck out successfully before, Steve?" I tried to keep the skepticism out of my voice.

"Oh, yeah. I just have to be careful. I'm on probation with her as it is." He looked sheepish.

"Wow. So, is this gonna be an okay thing, or. . . . ?"

I knew it wasn't my job to counsel people out of sessioning with me, but I have this weird thing about not wanting to mess up marriages. God knows enough of them go up in flames without my help. There's just something about the idea of such a crushed hope—the euphoria and optimism people feel when they walk down the aisle—and then what an excruciating memory that must be when they're meeting angrily in divorce court later on. I didn't want any part of it.

"I don't know," Steve went on. "I'm kind of hitting a bottom with this stuff. I think I'm a sex addict. It's been like this for the last few years, but my compulsions seem to be coming to a head lately."

"Hm." I thought for a minute. "I don't mean to say that you should, but have you ever thought about checking out one of those Sex Addicts Anonymous types of meetings?" I realized it had to sound weird coming from me, but I liked Steve and I'd heard that those meetings helped people sometimes.

"Oh, I've already got a meeting directory in my briefcase. I'll be going in the next few days."

"What do you want to do, then?"

I looked at the tightly-wound man sitting next to me on the over-stuffed love seat and wondered what the hell we were up to. I have to admit, I wanted to go on our little excursion now more than ever. I wanted to find out what it was like to hang out with a man who was having his own sexual hurricane. How long would it take us to blow through town and what would be left after we were done? I was so engrossed in the idea of this potential marathon of wrongness that it barely registered at first when he mentioned Mistress Barbarella in the same conversation.

" . . . We might pick her up on the way; I don't know. We'll see how it goes . . ." Steve was saying.

*Wait a minute. He wants someone else to join us? And a mistress at that?* I knew that a lot of pro dommes would frown upon the kind of liberty-taking I liked to do in my sessions. For most of the women in this business, I was pretty sure that the line between professional BDSM and conventional types of sex was a rigid one. And even though I'd told Steve that I just wanted to watch at the swinger's party, I had started to feel some curiosity about what it might be like to do a little mingling as well. I didn't want some tight-assed, self-appointed authority figure coming in and setting up professional boundaries. I resolved to try to keep Steve sufficiently distracted that night so that he wouldn't even remember to call her.

"Anyway," Steve continued, "I should get going so I'm home in time for dinner. I'll call you Saturday."

He clapped a friendly hand on my knee and then used it for leverage to hoist himself up off the couch. Without a glance in my direction, he took off at a stiff march, not even giving me enough time to say a parting word.

"Good-bye, Steve," I said anyway.

As I walked back to my hotel, I thought about how hard it must be for Steve, and for his wife. I knew what it was like to be him, to have compulsions that would not be ignored, compulsions that had nothing to do with the ability to truly love someone who didn't share them. But I knew how I would feel if I were Mrs. Steve, too. I wouldn't be able to help but feel betrayed, rejected by his need for the company and stimulation of other women, as if, whatever I was, it was simply not enough. Filled with conflicting emotions as I made my way through the midtown Manhattan crowds that late afternoon, I said a little prayer about Steve and his situation.

*Please God, don't let him get to one of those Sex Addicts Anonymous meetings before we have a chance to go through with our session Saturday night. Amen.*

• • •

"So I need to be on my way back to the hotel no later than four," I said, getting into Steve's car. It was almost two in the morning, and he had just picked me up. We were starting later than we'd expected, because his wife had taken longer to fall asleep than usual.

"No problem. We'll pick up Barbie. The party's pretty close to where she is anyway."

Crap. It was too late; he'd already made official plans with Mistress Barbarella. Not knowing what else to do, I tried to prepare myself with some preliminary information.

"What's this Barbie like, anyway? I mean, is she gonna come in here and try to run everything, or . . . ?"

"No, no, Barbie's really cool," Steve waved a hand at me. "I've known her forever; she was actually the first professional domme I ever saw for sessions. She's this little blond Byelorussian powerhouse."

"Hmm . . ."

"Don't worry, I told her about you. I told her you're more of a regular person than a passive slave-girl type. It'll be fine, you'll see."

I pictured a blond Paulina Poriskova folding herself haughtily into the car, motioning me into the back seat matter-of-factly. *She'll probably turn the whole goddamn night into the Barbie show.*

"Now," Steve said as he pulled into a curb in front of a brick building a few minutes later, "I'm afraid I need to ask you to get into the back seat."

*Exactly,* I thought crossly, and waited to roll my eyes until I was out of the car. Steve sensed something anyway.

"Sorry. It's just that she's pretty pregnant and needs the room," he said as I climbed in behind him.

Did he just say *pregnant?* I was momentarily speechless. It's not like I'd never been around pregnant ladies before, and I'd even known a couple of dommes who'd done sessions right up until their last week before delivery. It's more that it threw off my whole cranky idea about her. Of *course* she should have the front seat, for starters.

A minute later, a hugely pregnant blond woman with remarkably plump lips and with a handsome young man at her side came up to the front passenger door.

"Okay. I see you in couple of hours," she said to her companion, in her thick and almost lazy-sounding Byelorussian drawl.

The blond boy, who couldn't have been more than twenty, smiled at us and waved as we pulled away.

"He's very upset," Barbie sighed as she pulled the seatbelt over her large belly. Her cell phone rang, and she cursed as she fumbled to pull it out of the bag she'd just set on the floor.

"Hello. No! You quit bothering me. I work now. I'm home in couple of hours, I told you."

She snapped the phone shut angrily. Her voice sounded like a drowning person struggling to make it to the surface. There was a lot of fight in it, but it was sluggish somehow, too. She turned to me, and I saw for the first time the softness of her face, even as there was something unyielding underneath. Steve had said she was in her mid-twenties, and she'd been doing this for a living since she was seventeen.

"Sorry about that." Her tongue wrestled with the "th" sound, making it almost its own syllable. "My boyfriend doesn't want me to, but I wanted me to come out with you tonight. I been cooped up so long. . . ."

"That's okay," I said, and was about to introduce myself when her phone rang again.

"Shit!" She spat the word at the little device in her hand, and then opened and snapped it shut without talking to whoever was on the line.

"Now wait, now that's not cool—" Steve jumped in.

"No, I don't care, he's being an asshole." Barbie threw the phone at her bag.

"He's the father of your baby! If he's upset, maybe we should go back," Steve tried again.

I found myself transfixed by the sound of Barbie's furious-yet-sleepy voice and Steve's attempt to argue for family values as we were on our way to a kinky sex party.

"I don't care. He's being a child. He knows I work now!" Barbie shouted half-heartedly. The phone rang yet again, and she cursed once more, but laughed this time as well.

"Barbie, you have to answer it and calm him down. You gotta make an effort to respect his feelings if it's going to work out. You're a family now," Steve counseled earnestly.

She sighed loudly and groaned as she bent over to retrieve the phone. Pointing out to her boyfriend that it was Steve who had insisted she answer his call, she half shamed, half soothed him into finally believing that the two of us had no plans to whisk her permanently away from him.

"My God!" she said after she hung up, sounding exhausted.

I thought about how much I liked the sound of her voice already, and knew I'd have called back several times myself, even if only to hear her shouting at me. I felt for her boyfriend, having to spend any time away from her.

"You smell really nice by the way," I blurted. "And I'm Marnie."

"Thank you," she turned to smile at me. "Really, I smell good? I was worried that I smell like dungeon, like sessions I just came from," she laughed shortly.

"No, seriously. You smell like a clean flower."

Barbie laughed again and looked at Steve, who reached over and patted her leg affectionately. She turned back to face me.

"So what you like to do at party tonight?"

"I don't know. Maybe just watch?" I shrugged.

"I'd like for you to have an orgasm," Steve looked at me in the rearview mirror.

"Yes, great!" Barbie clapped her hands.

I wondered when Steve had changed his mind about just using me to get through the door, but didn't hold the change against him. I just wasn't sure how effective I'd be in an unfamiliar setting.

"That sounds nice and all, but what happens if I get performance anxiety or something?" I'd never had an audience larger than two or three people.

"No, no. No pressure! We help you." Barbie looked at me reassuringly, and Steve nodded.

*Jesus,* I thought. *Am I really about to get paid three hundred dollars an hour for letting a woman as gorgeous as Barbie help me come?* Settling into the faded leather of Steve's backseat, I smiled at the beautiful skyscrapers and ugly mountains of sidewalk trash outside my window, and had the random thought that this particular night alone would make up entirely for having been a virgin until the age of twenty.

"You girls okay to wait here while I park?" Steve stopped the car just inside a parking garage.

"Yes. You park and come back."

Barbie opened the passenger door and heaved her belly around to face the outside. I got out and followed her to the sidewalk. Steve caught up to us, and we hurried down the street toward an unmarked building. I surprised myself by getting a sudden case of nerves. Sometimes even normal parties made me a little shy. What if my small-talk abilities deserted me entirely in the face of a bunch of strangers all nuding out around me at once? Would casual sex on a massive scale be any less awkward than casual conversation sometimes was?

"I don't want to be clingy," I said, "but I'd like to stick with you guys at this thing."

"Of course you stay with us. We not here to socialize."

Barbie sounded cross, but not with me. It was like she was already preparing to fend off anyone who tried to invade, like a mother lion ready to swat away ill-mannered hyenas. She was several years younger than I, but she reminded me of what it was like when I'd been in third grade and some older, confident teenage girls from the neighborhood used to take me to matinees. It was like having all the protection of being with an adult, but none of the potential for getting in trouble. I half wondered if Barbie was going to grab my hand at some point. I made sure to walk within her reach.

• • •

"Put your clothes in here with ours, Marnie."

Steve held open a small locker. We were in the bathroom area of the large apartment where the party was being held. We'd passed two rooms with clusters of naked people scattered throughout on our way in. There was a washer and dryer outside the shower where the three of us stood, and I could feel steam settling on my bare stomach as I pushed my jeans and sweater into the already full cubby hole. Someone must have rinsed off right before we got there.

Steve was naked except for some leather contraption he'd fastened around himself for the purpose of maintaining his erection. I'd stripped down to a simple black pair of thigh-highs and heels, and Barbie had changed into a tiny leather bikini that barely covered her swollen breasts and the small triangle of blond beneath her bulging stomach.

"Ohhh, how pretty!"

She smiled and took one of my nipples between her thumb and forefinger. Her fingers were cool on my skin, and she smiled down at my breasts like they were personal friends of hers.

"Thank you."

I stared down at the manicured nails caressing my hardened nipples. I was afraid that if she looked directly into my eyes right then, she would see that they'd spun around in my head and come up dopey red hearts.

"Okay, let's go—we gotta get Marnie home before she turns into a pumpkin."

Steve steered us abruptly toward a small room near the front door. There was a raised bondage table about the size of a single bed, a spanking horse, and a couple of small couches. A party of three was busy on one of the couches. I couldn't decide whether it was impolite to look or uptight of me to look away.

Although the lighting was dim, I felt a pang of insecurity as I surveyed the little orgies going on around me. Most of the men were average-looking, but many of the women were thin in that New York way, as if they haven't hit puberty yet except for a growth spurt. I'm not an overweight person, but I'm much curvier than a fourth grader. I sucked my stomach in tighter as Steve motioned me over to the spanking horse. I climbed aboard and made myself comfortable. There were places to rest my hands and feet on either side, and my body sank into the soft leather padding as Barbie started caressing my back while Steve fiddled with some stuff in his bag.

"You tell us what's okay, yes?"

She stepped away as Steve came over with a gloved hand and a small bottle of lubricant. I nodded my head and waited. Steve slipped first one and then two lubed fingers inside me. I gasped and shut my eyes. It was all so sudden. One minute we're making conversation in a clanky old elevator, the next minute I'm letting someone's hand all up in my business in front of a small crowd of strangers. I turned to look for Barbie in an attempt to focus on something besides self-consciousness, and saw her taking a small paddle out of Steve's bag.

"We warm you up first, eh?" Barbie let out a short groan as she knelt beside me.

First they wanted me to come, now they wanted me to submit to some actual S/M stuff, too? It was more "work" than I'd been expecting, but not unreasonable, really. And I had a gut feeling that Barbie would be good to me while I subbed to her. Steve was still massaging my insides when she moved behind me and directed him out of the way. As soon as he removed his fingers, she brought the small leather paddle to my ass, rubbing it in slow circles on each of my cheeks. The tickle of her gentle caresses with the paddle made me laugh.

"Funny, eh? Is supposed to be punishment."

She feigned sternness, more for the benefit of the few people who stood around watching than for me. She started spanking me with the paddle, and I hid my face in the warm leather of the spanking bench in the hopes that I would appear to be taking this more seriously than I actually was. I don't generally like to fake a scene. I don't like the implication that it's not authentic kink unless someone's actually being hurt, and hence you better make it look that way if that's not what's really happening. But as Barbie continued to spank me a little harder, I couldn't help but make noises to seem like it was really *punishment*. I thought it was what she wanted, and I wanted desperately by that point to give her something she wanted.

When the paddling stopped, I turned to see Barbie pulling a leather harness out of Steve's bag. As she pulled it on, I noticed that there was not an imperfect ripple or bulge anywhere on her body. Her tanned skin was smooth and tight over every curve, and even her heavy stomach looked like something out of a Vargas painting.

As I turned back around to wait for her, a penis appeared several inches in front of my face. A warm hand took one of mine and placed it gently on the semi-erection. *What is the etiquette at a place like this?* The penis in my hand wasn't a bad-looking one, but I wasn't sure I liked the feeling of being some stranger's drive-up teller at the hand-job bank. Just then, Barbie began rubbing something blunt and smooth between my legs.

"I'm sorry, I need this back now," I apologized to the man's waist, and removed my hand. I figured I would need to be able to brace myself.

"This is okay?" Barbie leaned forward and whispered in my ear.

"It's great," I whispered back.

Grunting quietly, Barbie entered me in one smooth, quick motion, with a nice-sized dildo she had covered in cold K-Y. I moaned, and she held my hips, beginning to thrust in and out, and on the fourth or fifth plunge, she flipped some switch that made the dildo begin to vibrate inside me.

"Oh my *God,*" I breathed into the cool leather beneath my face, and began pushing back into her every time she shoved forward.

Almost as abruptly as she'd entered me, Barbie pulled out and went to lean against the bondage table.

"Sorry. I get tired so fast now," she told me, trying to catch her breath.

"That's okay," I said, and meant it. Much as I'd loved having her inside me, there was no way I could come in that position anyway. There was no point in working the poor girl to death.

"Why don't we have her sit back on one of the couches?" Steve said to Barbie, and helped me off the spanking horse.

Barbie took a towel from Steve's bag and draped it over the worn brown cushions of the nearest sofa. A naked woman was wrapped around the lap of a naked man at the far end of the couch, and they both turned to watch us. I slipped the first two fingers of my right hand into my mouth and then pressed them between my open legs. Barbie sat down next to me and took one of my nipples into her mouth. I leaned my head back and shut my eyes as she and I both worked away on my body. As I tried to concentrate, I could feel the urgency of the pulse beneath my fingers receding, and I tried to coax it back with thoughts of Barbie's hand and paddle. *What if it takes me too long? What if Barbie gets tired, or Steve gets bored? Would he want me to fake an orgasm, to at least put on a show?* I had never faked an orgasm in my life, and had no desire to start doing so. Did that make me a bad worker?

I knew I was going to need some help.

"Barbie, do you think—would you mind—there's this one thing that helps me finish quickly, but I don't want you to do it if you're uncomfortable."

"Wonderful. Tell me." Her drowsy eyes lit up and she leaned in toward me.

"I just need you to massage my, um, G-spot while I touch myself. It's hard for me to reach it with my own hand."

"Okay." She stood up to grab some gloves and the lube. Steve stretched out on the floor at her feet, staring intently. "I never done this before. Where is this gee spot?" Her lips tickled my ear.

"You just bend your fingers like this"—I took my free hand and curved the index and middle fingers together in a C-shape—"and then rub them on the inside wall that's closest to you."

Barbie began feeling around inside me, searching my face expectantly for signs that she was in the right place.

"Up a little more, please . . . yeah . . . like that, right—*mm*, right there exactly."

"*Mmm,* yesss," Barbie echoed me with her own excitement.

This time when I closed my eyes I was able to shut out everything except that feeling bringing me closer and closer to release. I forgot about the people at the other end of the couch, about Steve, about whatever I might or might not look like as I sat next to this gorgeous woman and tensed every muscle in my body before letting go. I held my breath as I felt it starting. I don't really make any sound on the way up. but when it hits, my body jerks forward and then slams hard against whatever piece of furniture I'm sitting or lying on. As Mistress Barbarella rubbed my insides with delicate precision and I rubbed my outsides with a final furious roughness, I kept my eyes shut and began convulsing on the couch. It felt like it went on for half an hour. I kept thinking I was done and then my body hit another peak, like waves crashing too close together inside me. Finally we both sat back, breathing heavily, our respective wrists lying limply at our sides. I looked down and saw that Steve had come as well. After a couple of minutes, Barbie got up to hand him some paper towels.

"We get cleaned up. You rest there until you ready, we wait for you." Barbie came up to me and took my face in her hands. She kissed each of my cheeks, and then put her mouth close to my ear again. "Thank you. Now I have new skill." She seemed genuinely pleased with herself and with me.

As Steve and Barbie disappeared down the hall, I waited for the strength to come back to my limbs.

Pulling up to my hotel a short while later, Steve reached a hand back toward me and when I grasped it, he pulled me forward so his lips could reach my palm. When he let me go, I clapped him warmly on the shoulder before turning to let myself out.

"Good call, bringing Barbarella along!"

He grinned at me. Barbie turned around to face me one last time.

"I know we just met and it's kind of rushing into things," I told her, "but I already love you. You don't need to say anything back," I held up a hand, "I'm just saying I love you. If you want to say you'll marry me of your own accord, that's your business."

Barbie looked pleased. "You know, you much cooler than I

thought you would be. Steve told me you a nice girl, but you nothing like what I expected."

I was still smiling when I got up to my room a few minutes later. I spoke to the ceiling before closing my eyes and slipping into a short but energizing sleep.

*Way to go with keeping him out of those meetings. I mean seriously. Amen.*

# THIRTEEN

"I'M SORRY, MARNIE, but I have to cancel our appointment for Wednesday. There's a big meeting at work that day and I can't get out of it."

It was the fourth such call in three days, and it finally dawned on me. *It's the first week of April. It's tax time.*

I don't know what I'd been thinking when I'd booked this trip for New York. I guess I had been on such a roll on the east coast that it never occurred to me to think about the bigger picture. I'd booked five sessions before even leaving Los Angeles, and had expected to fill up the rest of my time easily after arriving. That's how it always worked. Now I had only one appointment remaining. My cell phone had not beeped with anything but cancellations and apologies since I'd gotten here.

I had two more full days and nights left. And I was getting grouchier by the minute from being cooped up in my hotel room with nothing to do. I realized it was really the first truly free time

I'd had in the city since I started coming. I was usually so busy with sessions that I saw only the inside of my hotel, the various session rooms, and whatever was visible from cab windows. My final appointment was scheduled for the next evening, so catching an earlier flight back to L.A. wasn't going to work. *Fuck it,* I thought. *I'm going to go and be one more tourist in Times Square tonight.*

As I set out from my hotel, I remembered that New York was actually having what amounted to a heat wave for that time of year. I'd been inside with the air conditioning for so many hours straight, I hadn't even thought about the weather in days. By the time I got to where I was going, I felt overdressed in my tank top and jeans. I also felt unexpectedly cheered up. What might have annoyed me in the summer time—overcrowded sidewalks full of warm, damp bodies bumping up against my bare arms—provided me instead with a contact high.

I scanned the faces of everyone I passed. The crowds were mixed in a way I never saw much of in most parts of L.A. Dark skin, lighter skin, all kinds of skin, and all of it slightly shiny like mine, from the effort of moving at a steady clip in the humidity that had come with the warmth of that week. There was a sensual beauty to every face I saw that night, and when too-young men and old guys alike smiled at me or murmured joking come-ons as I passed, I couldn't help but smile back at each of them as I kept moving. I had no destination in mind. Maybe I'd just walk around until I was tired enough to go back to the hotel. Or maybe—*Wait a minute, is that . . . ?*

"Todd Bridges?" I finished the thought out loud.

The man I thought was Todd was walking past me on the sidewalk. There were people in between us, though, and I was surprised when his head turned. I hadn't thought there was any chance that he'd hear me. He looked warily in my direction: *another fan, smile politely, don't slow down.* I understood. After his childhood years on the sitcom *Diff'rent Strokes* and then his very public struggles with drugs and the law in the early 1990s, he probably got recognized a lot on the street. I raised a hand and smiled politely back. I wasn't sure that he would remember me, anyway.

"Oh my GOD!" he yelled, and broke away from the man he'd been walking with. He zigzagged his way through the people between us, and lifted me off my feet in a hug when he reached me.

"Oh my God!" he said again, "Joan, baby, I can't believe it! What are you doing here?!" His friend, a cute Italian-looking guy about my height, came over to us and smiled in bewilderment. "Dude, this is my *buddy,* I haven't seen her in *years,* I can't *believe* it! We were in rehab together in Los Angeles! Oh my *God!*" he exclaimed again, and picked me up a second time.

"Okay, okay," I said, laughing, as he let me back down to the sidewalk.

I was not only relieved that he remembered me, but gratified by his enthusiastic welcome. Suddenly it felt like a vacation instead of a failed business trip.

"So what are you doing here, how've you been, do you live here now, what's goin' *on?*" Todd spoke rapidly and then put a hand on his friend's shoulder before I could answer. "This is my friend Mike. Mike, this is Joan. We met in rehab in L.A.!" And then he gave me an exaggerated once-over, walking a complete circle around me. "*Damn,* you look *good,* girl."

"Thanks," I said. "I guess the last time you saw me, I looked pretty different." We both laughed, and his friend raised an eyebrow.

"This girl used to be as bald as me!" Todd rubbed a hand over his shaved skull.

"No way, really?" Mike seemed to find the news impressive.

"I'd always wanted to see what it felt like, and since I wasn't working at the time or trying to date anybody, it seemed like the only chance I might ever get," I explained.

Not only had I shaved my head in rehab, but I'd put on a fast thirty pounds as well, only a few of which I technically needed. I took to wearing oversized T-shirts and a pair of my dad's sweatpants, and got mistaken in the hospital elevator one day for a thirteen-year-old boy. It was no wonder Todd was still looking at me with a certain amount of shock. I had long brown hair now, real makeup on my face, and a pushup bra underneath my clingy white tank top. He, however, looked just as cute as I'd remembered him.

"Listen, it was nice to meet you, but I told Jeanie I'd be home by ten." Mike reached out to shake my hand and turned back to Todd.

"Okay," Todd said, hugging his friend quickly. "I'll call you tomorrow morning."

"Great. We'll be by to pick you up at eleven." Mike waved, walking away.

"Aren't you with him?" I asked, confused.

"Nah, Mike's my friend from way back. He lives out in Jersey with his wife and kids. I'm staying at the W Hotel, just a couple blocks from here."

"Cool!" I said.

Todd looked at me, pleased. "I came to town to do a spot on BET, and that's where they stashed me. You gotta see my room," he said, and pulled me toward the street corner.

"Come check this out!" Todd yelled excitedly from near the television console.

I stopped sniffing the expensive, still-wrapped bar of soap (lavender, it turned out) and put it back in its elegant dish, and went to see what Todd wanted to show me in the other room.

"Look at this. Look what's in here!" He opened the minibar and pulled out a small drawer at the bottom. He fingered different items in the fridge—Godiva chocolates, old-fashioned eight-ounce glass bottles of Coke, high-end bottled waters, midget carafes of fine wine. From a drawer he pulled other goodies—an adorable miniature sewing kit, a jar of macadamia nuts, a cellophane-wrapped pair of terry cloth slippers, an "intimacy kit," complete with three condoms (one of them flavored) and a cute little tube of lubricant. "And I can have all of this if I want, they're paying for everything!"

I stared at him for a few seconds. "God*dammit,* I love you."

"What did I do?" he asked, laughing. I shook my head, not sure how to explain.

He had been on crack, had been to jail, had guns held to his head, had lost everything. And here he was now, looking like the nine-year-old Willis again from *Diff'rent Strokes,* beside himself over little luxuries that most people in his current position of relative celebrity would barely notice, much less get this happy about.

I was happy about it, too, about the whole thing—getting dumped by all those clients so that I ended up in Times Square and in this room, looking through this minibar with Todd Bridges. I'd had a crush on him when I was little and he was on TV. We'd both grown up to be drug addicts, both had gone to rehab; and somehow, despite slim odds, we had both stayed clean long enough to make it here, to the W, during a fantastic heat wave in the middle of tax season in New York. If he hadn't told me he was married, I'd have grabbed him right then and there.

I woke up to the sound of my cell phone ringing the next morning.

"Hi, is this Marnie?"

"Yes, this is she," I answered.

"This is Ron. I'm calling to confirm our appointment for five thirty this evening."

"Oh!" I had all but decided that this last guy wasn't even going to bother canceling, but was simply going to blow off the appointment altogether. "Okay, sure, that's great. I'm in room three forty-eight, and if you just want to call me when you're in the lobby so I know who's knocking . . ."

"Sure, no problem. I'm looking forward to it," Ron said, and hung up.

I wasn't necessarily looking forward to it myself. He had called me a couple of months earlier, after he'd seen my Web site, but before I had planned my next trip East. All he wanted to do was kiss and lick my feet. It sounded easy, but not terribly erotic. So what if my feet might be sopping wet with his saliva at some point. If that was the worst that happened, it would be an easy couple of hundred dollars in my pocket. I had suggested we meet in my hotel room rather than W's dungeon space, partly because it seemed more practical for a session where I would basically just need a comfortable place to sit, and partly because it meant keeping the money I would otherwise have paid out in a rental fee. W wanted me to call her before and after the session, for security's sake, and I had given her Ron's name and phone number, and told him I was doing so. I wasn't worried about anything except having enough towels on hand to dry my feet when we were through.

"*Whoa,*" I whispered and sunk against the wall, having just gotten a glimpse of Ron through the peephole.

All I'd been able to see at first was a bow-shaped pair of lips above a strong, smooth chin. When he looked down at his feet as he waited for me to open the door, I saw a gorgeous pair of puppyish brown eyes and a head of short, wavy brown hair. He was beautiful. I shivered at the thought that I had almost not put on lipstick out of boredom.

"Hi," I said, hoping my sudden nervousness wasn't evident.

"Hi, it's nice to meet you," he said.

I could tell he was nervous, too. He cleared his throat, then looked quickly away as he moved from the doorway into the room.

"Would you like to sit and talk for a minute before we start?" I motioned to the other double bed as I sat down on the one closest to me.

"Yeah, that'd be great." He gave a shy laugh and sat down.

We looked at each other silently for a few seconds. He held my gaze for the first time, and I felt both of our jitters dissolve into something else as we continued to stare without talking. Finally, I spoke up.

"I haven't done a foot fetish session before. Where would you like me to sit?"

"You can stay there if you want. I can lie down on the floor beneath you and hold your feet from that angle if that's okay with you."

"Sure," I said, "but I'd like you to undress before you get in position."

Ordering him to take his clothes off gave me an instant buzz. Yes, there was definitely something to being the one in charge.

After taking off his Levi's, plain white T-shirt, and boxers, Ron scooted into place underneath my feet. He put both his hands around my left calf and squeezed gently.

"*Mm*," he told me, "you look great, by the way."

"Thank you."

I'd worn a black pushup bra and matching panties and nothing else. He had requested that my feet be bare from the start. As his fingers moved down to my heel, then my sole, and finally my toes, I closed my eyes and lay back on the bed. Ron's hands provided the perfect amount of soft pressure for my tender size sevens, and when he started to use his mouth on first one foot and then the other, I became instantly addicted. Instead of sloppy and wet, his lips and tongue left my toes tingling and warm. He used his teeth to lightly nibble on the thickest parts of my heels, and I sat up to watch him.

"Your feet are so clean, so beautiful, Mistress," he murmured. His closed his eyes then, and I watched as his erection grew and came to rest against his abdomen.

It didn't do anything for me when he called me *Mistress,* but he seemed so turned on by thinking of me that way that I didn't want to spoil anything by requesting that he use just my name. Relaxing even more into my role as the director of this little scene, I moved my right foot down Ron's torso and brought it to within an inch of his cock.

"Oh God, Mistress!" he moaned, and pushed his pelvis off the floor.

He opened his eyes and stared into mine, his mouth still working its way from one end of my left foot to the other. I smiled down at him, and slid my right foot closer and closer, until my toes just touched his firm tip. As Ron began to moan louder, taking all five of my left toes into his mouth, I responded by running the sole of my right foot up and down what was now his visibly pulsing cock.

"Mm . . . God . . . Oh—Mistress—*Oh God may I please come now, Mistress?*" he begged, eyes still locked on mine.

I nodded once, then he bucked his hips and came loudly on the floor. I glanced at the clock as I waited for Ron's breathing to slow at my feet. Only fifteen minutes of our one-hour session had passed. I wondered what he would do now.

"Mistress, may I go to the washroom to clean up?" he requested.

"Absolutely."

I watched him pad across the carpet in his bare feet and close the bathroom door behind him. He was as gorgeous from the back as he was from the front—slender hips, muscular legs, and a nicely rounded ass that moved rhythmically as he walked.

"So, um, do I have to go now?" He looked at me uncertainly when he came back into the room.

I laughed, relieved and happy that he might not want to leave. "Of course, you don't have to go! You told me an hour. I think that entitles me to about forty-five more minutes," I teased.

"Okay," he grinned, and came to stand in front of me. "What would you like me to do for you, now?"

I thought about it for a second. "Well, how would you feel about letting me cane you? Not hard, more as a sensual type of thing?"

"I would let you do anything you wanted to," he assured me.

"Really?" I asked seriously, and reached a hand out to touch his firm stomach.

He looked up and into my eyes. "Yeah. I feel like I can trust you."

I was flattered by his impression of me but even more pleased with having made another person feel so safe. It was a heady feeling, and it made me like being on this side of things more than I would have thought possible.

"Well, then, why don't you lie down here on your stomach"—I stood up and motioned to where I'd been sitting on the bed—"and I'll get my cane."

Seeing Ron's beautiful, smooth ass waiting for me when I came back was almost too much to take. I hadn't realized it before then, but it seemed like I had an ass fetish that went both ways—I liked having mine played with and now I was hungry to play with his. I climbed into the middle of the bed and sat cross-legged next to

Ron's outstretched body. I ran my hand over his skin, from the middle of his back down over his cheeks and onto the backs of his thighs. He sighed, and I picked up the cane a client had brought me as a gift.

"I'm gonna start super-light, and stay pretty light the whole time, but I want you to tell me if at any point it's just not working for you—whether it stings or you're bored or anything else."

Ron laughed quietly. "I know I won't be bored."

"Okay." I smiled to myself. "But I do want you to let me know how you're feeling."

I put my left hand against the small of his back and began caning him lightly, across the center of both cheeks. I kept tapping at the same light level but started moving the cane slowly up, and slowly back down, so that I was covering a good two thirds of his bottom. Ron moaned softly and turned to watch me, his hands folded under his chin.

"That's so relaxing, it's almost hypnotic."

I set the cane aside and rubbed the area I'd been tapping. "Good."

I took the cane and resumed the rhythmic pace, but this time I made every fourth stroke slightly harder than the others. After a while of this variation, I switched so that every time the cane landed, it was with the same light sting as only one of them had been before. Keeping Ron at that intensity for a good five minutes, I stopped again and rubbed him gently where he had started to turn a light shade of pink.

"How are you doing?"

"Great, Mistress. Thank you." He was looking definitely dreamy.

During the next half hour, I took Ron from a totally painless tapping up to a level of intensity that was pretty impressive for someone who'd never taken—nor sought—any kind of corporal punishment before. I stopped regularly to massage his skin and ask how he was doing, and it seemed from his reaction as though he almost couldn't feel the sensations increase as we went along. When our time was almost up, I put the cane down for good and rubbed my hands over his skin while we talked.

"So, I'm curious—did you like that at all, or were you just humoring me?"

Ron looked thoughtful. "Well, at first it was just nice to be so close to you, and since it didn't hurt at all, I liked it in that sense. But then when you started to do it a little harder, and then a little harder than that, I started to feel like I *wanted* you to keep on. But I honestly don't know if I was actually craving the caning or whether it just felt so good when you rubbed me between strokes that I never wanted that to stop."

"That's great," I said, and leaned down to kiss his back. Of all the people I could have ended this trip with, I was glad it was him.

"Thanks!" He stretched his neck toward me and kissed my knee.

I leaned down again to kiss his shoulder. As I was halfway up again, he turned his face to mine and simply stared. I moved slowly back down to him. He stayed still while I kissed his cheek, but moved his mouth onto mine when I was done. Before I knew it, I was on my back and he was on top of me, his hips pressing lightly against mine, as we caressed each other on the bed. It felt like forever since I had really kissed anyone, let alone anyone who was this good at it. Ron's lips were supple and his tongue teased mine, touching me just enough to make me stretch toward him for more. He ran his hands over my sides and hips, but seemed hesitant to touch my bra or between my legs. As turned on as I was, I was glad he was so reserved. I was sure he would be fun to have sex with. It was just that I was enjoying this so much, I didn't want it replaced by anything else just yet.

I don't know how long we stayed like that, but he did finally have to leave.

"I'm sorry," he said, "I told a friend I'd come by for a little while. I wish I'd known how much I'd like you. I would have told him I was busy."

"That's okay. I should finish packing up my stuff, anyway, and make it an early night. My plane leaves practically at the crack of dawn."

I watched him as he pulled on his clothes.

"Thanks for seeing me today. Really. It was way better than anything I had imagined." He smiled.

"Me, too," I said seriously.

In the hours after our ninety-minute whirlwind romance, I thought about Ron again and again. Although I didn't think being a domme was anything I would ever seek out more aggressively, I was glad I'd had the experience, and not just because Ron had turned out to be such a dreamboat.

I knew what I had done with him didn't fit what other people might think of as domination—especially the part where I had jerked him off with my foot and then made out with him to my heart's content. A lot of Mistresses would consider it whorish, an amateur's attempt to claim control where only sexual service really existed. I didn't care. I felt like by that point I deserved the relief I had found, in realizing that I could be turned on by someone who wasn't dominant himself. It had been so long since I'd had a hot, deeply submissive experience of my own, that without this new-found pleasure in topping, I wouldn't know if I was kinky at all anymore. Sure, I'd had some incidents with dominant women lately that had been fun, but none of them had generated the types of feelings in me that T had, back before the whole thing went south. Even the time with Marcus, all those months before, seemed lukewarm compared to the fire I remembered with T. I wondered what T would think if he could have seen me telling Ron to strip, or getting him to take his first caning. The idea of T thinking of me at all, or looking at me like he used to, made my throat ache suddenly, and I pushed the thought away. Whatever that had been with T, it hadn't been what I wanted. I knew that much for sure.

Sitting in my window seat the next morning as the plane taxied down the runway, I smiled as I remembered that first electric moment when Ron's lips had touched mine. I wondered if it would be possible to meet anyone like Ron at home, outside of session, and whether I'd actually want to date a guy like that. Could I be happy with a boyfriend who was cute, hot for me, and a good kisser, even if he wasn't kinky in the same way I was? I didn't know.

Whatever the case, I felt hopeful about my personal life for the first time in a while. Yet underneath, I felt something else that I tried immediately to ignore—something hollow inside me, like a wish that had folded in on itself until it no longer took up any space at all.

# FOURTEEN

**I ALMOST PASSED** on Jake altogether, based on our first conversation. In describing what he wanted to do with me, he sounded not so much like he didn't know as that he didn't much care.

"I was thinking about spanking, maybe a little bondage too," he said in a near monotone.

"Okay. Just so you know, my donation is three hundred dollars per hour for light-to-medium sessions," I said.

He wanted me to come to his hotel room in the City of Commerce, and I half hoped that my higher fee for outcall sessions would be more than he was willing to spend.

"That's fine. Can you come in an hour or so?"

"Actually, I can't come until early evening," I answered.

Maybe the timing would be the deal-breaker? I crossed my fingers. He didn't sound unpleasant, and he didn't want to do anything that was out of bounds—I just felt a little bored. But since I hadn't done any sessions since I'd gotten back from New York, I couldn't quite rationalize saying no from an economic perspective. When he said early evening was fine, I got his room number and hopped in the shower.

The drive to meet him felt like a trip halfway to Death Valley, although it was really just a few minutes south of downtown L.A. The City of Commerce is a slew of blocky buildings splayed out on the side of Interstate 5 like cargo that's fallen off the back of a semi on its way to San Diego. It looked neither like a city nor a hub of commerce. It gave me a parched feeling just driving by it.

After parking in the mostly vacant hotel lot, I made my way through the completely empty lobby and into the elevator. The air in the place smelled like shit-scented cigars and months-old Marlboro smoke, and I tried not to inhale too deeply as I rode up to Jake's fifth-floor room. I willed myself to look interested as I knocked and waited for him to answer.

"Hi."

A cute and boyish face smiled around the edge of the door, then disappeared behind it. The door swung all the way open and I stepped inside. I will say, it perked me up a little that Jake turned out to be nice-looking. He was a lot taller than me—a good foot at least—with straight, almost shaggy, short brown hair and a strangely innocent-looking face for his age. That's what had made me see him as boyish, initially. He was clearly my age or a little older, but his brown eyes were slightly wider and his smile was somehow both shy and eager at the same time.

"It's nice to meet you," I said, and put my bag down, in case he wanted to shake hands.

When he nodded at me, still smiling but saying nothing, I took the bag over to one corner of the unmade bed and set it down. He followed me into the room and sat on the opposite edge of the bed. In my daydreams I often imagined that the perfect partner would be a man who had very little to say, hence lowering his chances of saying something irritating and spoiling my ability to tolerate his company long enough to complete a sex act. As Jake brought my daydreams to life, I realized that, in reality, I often counted on the sometimes pointless chatter of men, clients in particular, to calm my own nerves when facing a new sexual situation. I preferred to play the reserved, mysterious role myself, but even a few seconds of silently staring back at Jake failed to generate anything on his end. Fidgeting with the interlocking zippers on my toy bag, I finally blurted out the first thing that popped into my head.

"Why would a person leave Vegas to gamble?"

He had mentioned in his initial e-mail that he lived in Las Vegas, and was in town for a poker tournament. His eyes shifted briefly to the crumpled blankets near his thigh, but his smile remained fixed and he nodded again.

"The tournament moves all over the world. I follow it wherever it goes," he said. "I'm a professional poker player. I've been on television a few times."

"Wow, that's cool," I said politely.

It did sound kind of neat, but it was a dead end as far as small talk went. I didn't know anything about poker or professional gambling, and could only continue looking agreeable. Finally I offered to show him what was in my bag.

"I brought two kinds of cuffs. I wasn't sure which one you would like better. These are leather, pretty easy and comfortable, and then these—" I pulled out the other "—are Velcro."

I set both pairs on the bed, and saw his long slender fingers reach out to pull them closer to where he was sitting. I stared into my bag as I heard him pulling at the Velcro and opening and closing the hooks that locked the cuffs to each other.

"I brought this paddle. It's pretty flexible, but stings a lot more than it looks like. This is a pretty soft flogger—my riding crop— some clothespins—and these are some pretty heavy clamps. I don't even know if I could take these today, as they're really intense. Also, just for the record, I have a hard time with the clothespins or the clamps directly on the tips of my nipples, which are really sensitive, and I just can't take much there."

I looked up then, and he nodded once more, staring at me, waiting.

"I usually accept the donation at the beginning of the session," I said.

He wordlessly removed his wallet from his pants and counted out three hundred dollars in twenties, then held them out to me. I cleared my throat again.

"I have to use the restroom before we start. Would you like me to undress in there, or come back out here and take off my clothes?"

He had told me on the phone that I didn't need to bring any lingerie or other sex clothes, that he wanted me naked from beginning to end once I was in his room.

"You can take your clothes off in there, and then open the door for me when you're ready. I'm going to start by using the cuffs to restrain you in the shower, if that's okay with you."

"Sure," I smiled, relieved.

He had asked the question softly, looking at me expectantly, as if my answer actually mattered. In addition to the pepper spray in my bag and the friend I'd told where I was going, little things like his simple concern helped me feel secure in this type of situation. I could tell a lot about how safe someone was as a domme by whether or not they showed any consideration for my feelings before we started.

As soon as I was ready, I pushed the wide bathroom door open. When I heard him get up from the bed, I took a quick glance at my reflection in the mirror and stifled a groan. *Which son of a bitch invented fluorescent lighting? I'm sure I'm better-looking than this.* At least it was a little dimmer over by the shower.

He had taken off his shirt but kept his casual beige slacks and brown loafers on. The shirt he'd had on—a pink cotton, button-down number—had made his upper half look almost puffy, as if he'd gone soft in the shoulders and around the middle. It was a shock to see his beautiful, tanned stomach and back, all lean and lanky, muscular like a teenaged boy who's just hitting puberty and not quite grown into wider shoulders. He moved to where I was standing and looked down at me. I looked down, too.

"Stand up here, one foot on each side."

He held onto my arm as I stepped up, and held me tighter as I stretched across so that I straddled the empty bathtub.

"Put your hands up here."

As I raised my wrists toward the curtain rod above my left side, he took my left hand and put one of the Velcro cuffs on. After fastening the other onto my right, he hooked them together over the top of the rod, so that my wrists hung above me and could not be lowered. I stole glances at my naked body in the mirror as he fiddled with something, his back toward me, at the end of the fake marble counter. At least this position made the muscles in my thighs stand out, and my back arch in a way that made my stomach look flatter and my ass look as high as it had been ten years before. Maybe there's something to be said for bathroom scenes after all.

When he turned around, he was holding two clothespins. He brought them toward my breasts, but then seemed to think of something and put them back down. He moved in close to me, and began to run his hands over my body, moving from my breasts and arms down over my stomach and the length of my legs. He bent down to caress my calves, and then ran his palms and fingers over my ass. I expected him to start with a warm-up, spanking me lightly as I stood there, then moving on to the paddle. Instead he continued to rub my skin gently, his eyes following his hands as they covered and uncovered different parts of me.

"You have really soft hands, sir," I said quietly.

"Yes. I do."

I looked sideways at his face to check out his expression. It had been a teasing thing to say, and seemed out of character, at least according to the impression I'd had of him up till then. But his face still had the same open, pleasant look that had been there from the beginning.

Picking up the clothespins again, he placed one on each of my nipples, pinching a very small amount of skin in each, which actually hurts more than taking a larger bite. I did what I always do when a new client hurts me more than I'd been expecting.

"May I ask you something, sir?"

"Yes."

"Would you be opposed to taking a larger amount of my skin in each clothespin? It would hurt less and I could take them for longer that way."

His hands dropped to his sides and he said nothing. In the stillness of the seconds that followed, I worried that I had made him feel inept by asking him to do something differently. Finally, he reached for a clean washcloth. He folded it over twice, and brought it up to my face.

"Open your mouth."

I did as he said, and he softly pushed a corner of the washcloth between my lips.

"Open wider."

I let him push it in further and then bit down to hold it in place when he told me to. I felt a tingling in the pit of my stomach, the beginnings of intense arousal. I don't know how to explain it. Being gagged as a response to something I actually said, as opposed to just a form of play we'd agreed to, would normally be pretty offensive to me. But there was just something so gentle, even polite, about Jake's manner as he positioned the washcloth. He acted like a person who intended to control every part of our exchange, but who also cared how everything felt to me. It was the kind of combination that most excited me.

It was also the sort of behavior that most unnerved me. I had an impossible time using the safe word (even if I'd been able to speak) with real dominant partners who were as sexy as Jake was, so I knew I was simply going to take whatever he ended up doing to me. Since I didn't yet know what that would be, I felt helpless in a way I hadn't for quite some time.

His hands returned to the sides of my breasts, where he stroked absently for a couple of seconds before dragging each of the clothespins off my nipples without opening them. The quick pinching ache of it made me moan briefly into the washcloth, and something in his body language gave me the sense he was pleased. A moment later, he turned and left the room, and I listened to myself breathing deeply as I stared at the aging white tiles and detachable showerhead with massage settings.

He carried an ice bucket with him when he returned, and when he brought the open bucket over to the tub, I thought he meant to rub cubes of ice on me, a common form of sensation play. Instead, he lifted the bucket behind me and tilted it, and I realized it was filled with ice water, not ice. As he slopped a good quart of it down my back, I tried to scream into the makeshift gag, but the impact of the freezing liquid on my torso evaporated the air from my lungs, and all I could manage was a couple of high pitched gasp-whimpers. He brought the bucket around toward my face, and I tried to say something in earnest then—*I can't have anything touching my face, I don't want water poured over my head*—but even I couldn't understand me through the bunched terry cloth in my mouth.

"Quiet."

He said it with amused affection, not irritation or even real bossiness. It was like he knew I was okay, he was making sure of it, and he was simply trying to calm me down. The fear I felt was of the roller-coaster variety—more adrenaline rush than concern. Now even that was changing into something else.

As he poured more of the ice water down my front, I again felt the reflex to cry out from the cold, and again my lungs wouldn't allow it. I panted and moaned instead, and thought *thank God* when he set the bucket down and picked up something else.

A loud crack echoed off the tiles of the shower as he landed the leather paddle on the left side of my ass. It would have hurt a lot anyway because of the force he put into it, but stung even more because of the wetness of my skin. I cried out in surprise, the sound muffled by the washcloth, and he struck me again on the opposite side. He dropped the paddle after just two strokes, and began to rub me where I'd been hit. I leaned into his hands gratefully and he rubbed me everywhere else as well.

After a couple of minutes he left again, and I heard the soft sucking sound of shoes being pulled off, and then change jingling in a pocket as his pants fell to the floor. He was completely nude when he came back in, and I couldn't help but stare. He held himself in his left hand and stroked rhythmically, and his perfectly proportioned cock fit the rest of his beautifully naked self so well that if my mouth hadn't been holding the washcloth, it would have been hanging open. He came over to where I waited and hoisted himself up behind me.

Straddling the tub, he put his arms around my middle and pulled me back into him. Dropping one hand, he used it to position his cock so that it lay in a straight line up my lower spine. He pulled me back against his body so that when he moved his hips, he could make friction between my back and his front. I pressed back into him as well, and moved with him as he held me tightly. His warm lips went to the back of my neck, and I moaned as he kissed me there, kissed behind my right ear, and rocked me slowly over the empty tub. I wanted him to come, but I hoped he wouldn't any time soon. Some people end the session once they have an orgasm, and at the moment I had no desire to get dressed and drive back home.

After pressing his lips into my shoulder and neck, and his cock into the small of my back for a few more minutes, he stepped down and picked up the ice bucket again. A lot of the water was gone, but some ice was still in there, and he leaned down to refill it from the faucet in the tub. When he was finished, he pulled the lever that switched the flow from tub to showerhead, and suddenly I was being doused in cold water again. I leaned my head back so the shower wouldn't spray my face, and he put a tender hand on my shoulder to guide me back to the middle of the stream.

I didn't think it would do any good to make begging sounds into the gag, as it was obvious that he was going to do exactly what he felt like doing, for as long as he felt like doing it. His preference seemed to be for just enough of something to make me moan or yell, and then to switch gears. He turned the shower off, and I caught my breath in the absence of the cold water on my skin.

He moved his soft hands up and down the length of my soaking body, and then turned to pick up the clothespins again. This time he placed them directly on the tips of each nipple. The burning was excruciating at first, but when he put a hand flat on my stomach and said *shh* in my ear, something in my nerve endings shifted and all I felt then was turned on.

"*Mm,*" he murmured, apparently feeling my body relax under his palm.

He pulled the clothespins off quickly, and grabbed the ice bucket before stepping into the tub once more behind me. I didn't know how much more I could take of ice water pouring down my back and front, and I was relieved when he set the bucket down between his feet and picked up a couple of cubes to rub on my slightly sore nipples and still-red ass. The combination of melting cold and the mild heat of his hands was soothing. I was just thinking *how nice* when he reached for another washcloth and folded a handful of ice into it, like he was making something to keep the direct sting of ice away from my skin. Instead he put the icepack between my legs, and when I jumped, he opened it so that he could hold the washcloth from underneath, pressing the melting ice directly onto my swollen private parts. I involuntarily jerked my hips forward, and he swayed with me, keeping his hand in place, whispering in my ear, "Quiet, *quiet.*" The obvious pleasure in his voice, which seemed to take in both of us, made me still.

I moaned as he held me that way for another minute, and he moaned softly too. When he finally took the ice away, I felt dazed and limp, and everything I felt from then on simply translated to *his touch,* whether he was using the riding crop hard and fast on the insides of my thighs, or putting the heavy clamps on my nipples while he counted out loud to forty-five and held me under the cold shower again. He always stroked me softly whenever he was done, and he stroked himself repeatedly, as well. No matter what he did, I never once wanted him to stop. It wasn't even a question anymore of having a hard time saying the safe word. The idea of not being touched by him felt worse than any sensation his hands brought to my body, and it was somehow both a familiar and a completely new feeling.

After a certain point he went into the other room, and I could hear his hand working away until he finished himself off. I wondered why he hadn't done it in front of me, but found his strange modesty as compelling as the rest of him. Before untying me, Jake turned the shower on again and made it warm, rubbing me one last time, through the stream of steamy water. After turning it off, he put his arms all the way around me and helped me down to the floor. Grabbing a dry towel, he wrapped it around me and pulled it snug, like a parent wrapping his kid who'd just stepped out of the swimming pool on a chilly afternoon. Once he'd tucked the large towel around me, he held me by the upper arms and kissed the top of my head. I leaned my forehead into his bare chest, and he pulled me in and hugged me for a long time.

"You can get dressed now if you want."

I was confused. It felt like I had just gotten there. "Has it really been an hour already?"

"Yeah," he laughed quietly, and, giving my arms one final squeeze, left me alone in the bathroom with my clothes.

*It's what you thought T would give you in the beginning, that's what's familiar.* It popped into my head on the drive home that night. Was it true? No, I decided. I had never thought T was someone who would hold me tight, or quietly steer me into some strange place where I was warm inside even with ice on my skin. It was the total lack of resistance to what was happening that was familiar, and the longing I felt for more—that was all. Both those things had happened when I first got involved with T. But after a short while, surrendering to T's control felt more like getting into a car accident than riding a roller coaster. Yes, it had also involved a sharp spike in adrenaline, but the shock had stayed with me for days and I could never tell right away how badly I was hurt inside.

I wanted to do another session with Jake, and the lack of control I had around making that happen was nowhere near as fun as the lack of control had been in his hotel room. I knew it was the part of this job that would make me quit some day in the not too distant future. Now that I knew what it felt like to be overwhelmed by sexually submissive feelings again without having to submit to things that troubled me, I wanted to find someone in real life to do it with all the time. The only thing Jake had in common with T was that neither of them was around. Even before the in-person meetings with T became unbearable, the fact that I would get so stirred up and then have no way to talk to him or see him in between was agonizing. It wasn't quite that bad with clients—I'd been working on my detachment skills since Phil, after all—but it wasn't how I wanted to spend the rest of my sexually viable years, either.

I wanted to see Jake again, but I wanted to see me out there looking for something real even more.

I ended up getting Jake before the other. He e-mailed me a few days after our first meeting: *The session was great and I'm going to be at the same place this coming weekend. I really liked how your ass looked, and I have decided to take you there.*

I read it a few times, making sure it actually said what I thought it said. He had included his cell phone number, and I called him a few minutes later.

"Saturday would work best for me. I should get done with the tournament by around ten o'clock that night, if you want to come over after that," he offered.

"Can I ask you about something you wrote?"

I figured I might as well just come out with it, since there hadn't seemed an easy way to transition into the subject.

"Sure."

"Did you, um . . . Were you talking about having anal sex with me?" I tried to keep both the anxiety and the pure glee out of my voice.

"Uh-huh." Jake's tone was neutral.

I wasn't even sure what I wanted to say to him about it. In theory, the idea thrilled me. I had known from the moment he stepped naked into that bathroom that I wanted to have sex with him, and when he had been behind me in that tub, I had wondered more than once what he would feel like in my ass.

In practice, however, anal-sex-gone-awry was all too easy a scenario to stumble into. It wasn't like regular fucking, for me. The slightest pain during entry made my muscles reflexively tense up, even if I was trying to relax. That always led to a torturous spasm that wouldn't go away even after the person pulled out; it had to run its course, which was usually about sixty seconds long. With Jake being as insistent on control as he was, I was afraid he would expect me just to take it, the same way I had taken everything so happily last time. What if he wouldn't see me unless I agreed to that?

As soon as the thought formed in my head, I knew why this thing with Jake had reminded me so much of T initially. T was the first person who had ever made me feel this good, and I had been afraid that it would stop if I objected too much to too many of the things he wanted to do to me. Despite my best efforts to stifle myself, it had ended anyway. After waking up one day and realizing that not only had everything been hurting worse and worse when we were together but also that I hadn't even had an orgasm with him in months, I finally had told T I couldn't see him anymore. He stated flatly that we never had to do anything I didn't want to do again. But it was too late for me. I hadn't known what drove me to walk away back then, when he was finally offering me what I had wanted from him all along. But now I understood it. I had been too disgusted with both of us—with myself for having acquiesced in the first place, and with him for having been a part of it. I didn't want to make the same mistake with Jake. Not because of how I wanted to keep feeling about him, but because of how I wanted to keep feeling about me. I knew what I wanted to say to him, then.

"Could we start slow, and could you go slow even after I'm, you know, sort of prepared? I haven't done it in a while, and I'm afraid it might hurt if you entered me really fast."

"No, I'm not interested in hurting you that way. We'll use lube, I'll go easy, it'll be fine, I'll take care of it."

He sounded exactly like he had when he'd first asked me if it was okay to tie me up in the shower, like everything I felt mattered to him, and like he would, indeed, be taking care of it.

"Why don't you call me when you're done with your poker game?" I suggested.

Jake's room was brighter this time and a little bigger. The heavy floor-length curtains were wide open, but the glare from the lamps inside made it hard to see anything outside the large windows except for a few fuzzy points of light in the distance. He had pulled the ugly brown and orange bedspread down to the foot of the queen-size that took up about a third of the room. The clean white sheets were slightly rumpled, and I wondered if they were as comfortable as they looked.

I walked over to a small couch by the windows and set my bag down. When I turned around, Jake was looking at me intently and moving closer to where I stood. He surprised me by using his slender, teenage-boy hands to unzip my jacket when he reached me. As he pulled the sleeves down my arms and tossed my jacket onto the couch behind me my body began to tingle all over. He continued to undress me, watching my face, pulling my long-sleeved tee over my head, unbuttoning my jeans, and pulling off my shoes and socks as I held onto his shoulder for balance.

"Good, no underwear, just like I said," he smiled at me.

He had told me not to have on a bra or panties under my clothes this time. He put his hands on the sides of my face and pulled me up to kiss him. Pressing his lips on first my mouth, then my chin, then each side of my mouth, then square in the middle again, he continued to hold my face, and then began to bump his hips against mine. When he stepped back to take his shirt off, I spoke up.

"Could I use the restroom?"

I usually took a few minutes before getting right into things, and his stripping off my clothes had happened so fast I hadn't had time to say anything. I didn't really want to stop, but I didn't want to have to stop in the middle of anything else either, and I knew I had to pee.

"Not right now." He finished undressing and started kissing me again.

As in our previous session, his polite sternness made my stomach flutter, especially in combination with his warm lips on my face. I could feel myself getting carried away, and pulled back for a moment.

"I'm sorry to—" I hadn't planned how to say it exactly. "I just like to get it out of the way because I don't like thinking about it," I said, and was about to finish with some clumsy reference to the donation, when he nodded and turned around without a word, pulled a small wad of bills from his discarded jeans pocket, and handed it to me.

"Thank you." I shoved it in my bag and turned back to face him.

"I'd like you to bend over the bed."

"Could I please use the bathroom first?"

"No."

He looked at me seriously with his large brown eyes, but I felt teased somehow, like he didn't really care if I went or not, but just enjoyed saying no to me as much as I enjoyed the feeling it gave me to hear it.

"The thing is, I'm just afraid I won't be able to relax as much as I need to if I have a full bladder."

He had moved behind me and had been pushing me slowly with his body toward the bed, but stopped then and laughed quietly.

"Okay, you can go."

I closed the door behind me and sat down on the cold toilet seat. I was so tense with nervous excitement that I had to turn on the water at the sink in order to actually let go now that I had the opportunity. I had the simultaneous urges to finish up as fast as I could and to stay indefinitely in that bathroom. My throat felt open from exhilaration, and yet it was hard to catch my breath too, as if my airways were too constricted for oxygen to pass down to my lungs. After closing my eyes for a few seconds, I felt like I had enough of a hold of myself, and went to rejoin Jake near the bed.

"Bend over here," he said, putting his hands on the backs of my shoulders and pushing my upper body onto the mattress. "Spread your legs a little more." He eased his thigh between mine and pushed them further apart. "Stay like that."

I nodded without saying anything and heard him pull open a nightstand drawer behind me. A second later I recognized the small pop of a K-Y cap, and then Jake was holding my cheeks open with one hand and pressing something cool and firm between them. My hips twitched forward, and Jake, having positioned the small dildo effectively, used his free hand to pull me back into it.

"Hold still," he ordered quietly.

But as he began to push it inside me, I couldn't hold still no matter how hard I tried. His familiar grip and that lovely voice made me forget everything I'd said about wanting him to go slow. I dug my palms into the soft sheets and pressed backwards, taking the whole thing in quickly.

Jake let go of the dildo and grabbed onto my shoulders with both hands, then bumped his pelvis repeatedly against me as he pulled me back and then pushed me forward, pulled back and pushed forward.

"Stand up now, and don't let it slip out," he said a short while later.

He took my left arm gently in his hand and helped me upright off the bed. The dildo had a slightly wider base, making it relatively easy to hold when I stood up and turned around to face him. I watched as Jake fished around inside my open bag for something. A few seconds later, he had pulled out the heavy clamps and placed them on the tips of my nipples almost before I could register what was happening.

"*Oh,* I'm sorry sir, I can't really take those there," I said in a rush, wanting to bring the sharp and sudden burning to an end as soon as possible.

"Take it," he said, almost whispering, fingering the chain that ran between the clamps. When I moaned, he leaned down to put his mouth closer to my ear. "*Take it.* I'll count to ten."

I felt my shoulders drop at the same time as the burning in my nipples seemed to vanish into thin air. I could still feel strong pressure there, but it was no longer uncomfortable.

"*Mm,*" I said, closing my eyes, as he pulled me into his arms.

He counted slowly to ten and then held me away from him so he could remove the clamps. I felt drunk, weightless, like there was nothing he could do with me at that point that I wouldn't enjoy. Jake turned me back toward the bed and bent me over again, this time telling me to put my knees up on the mattress instead of standing with my legs on the floor. I dropped my head and chest down, and became suddenly nervous about my ass in the air. His cock was a lot bigger than the dildo he was pulling out of me. I heard the crinkling of a condom wrapper tearing open, and before I could voice my fears, he was pushing himself inside of me.

"Oh gosh, could you please, uh—" but he cut me off before I could say *go slowly.*

"*Shhh, shhh,*" he whispered, holding my hips with both hands and moving slowly, anyway, deeper inside.

And then he was all the way, painlessly, inside me, massaging internal bundles of nerves that seemed inconsistent with the regular function of that area. It was like I had an extra G-spot or something inside my ass. I sank my upper body all the way into the mattress as he thrust slowly in and out of me, and I closed my eyes as his movements lulled me into an almost dream-like state.

"Would you let me fuck your vagina?"

My head snapped back and my eyes popped wide open; I was glad Jake couldn't see my face from his position behind me. *Did he just use the word* vagina*?* I had never heard anyone say that during a sexual encounter. I had never *wanted* to. It always had the resonance, for me, of caveman gruntings, like it had been made up back when people barely knew how to string ungainly sounds together. But I have to admit—hearing Jake use the word, especially as part of such a welcome request, made me like him even more. Who *was* this poker-playing, usually silent, hot-bodied, "vagina"-dropping man for God's sake? I couldn't fathom what made him tick.

"Could you use a new condom?" I asked, turning to look at him.

"Oh, of course," he said, and detached himself to make the change.

When he was ready, he came back and tugged lightly on my ankle. "I want you to roll over on your back now."

As I wrapped my legs around his hips a second later and moved beneath him, he began a steady stream of murmurings in my ear, more than I would have ever expected to hear from him.

"You love feeling me inside you. You need it to be big enough so you can feel it, that's good, you're so good, your vagina belongs to me now. Your vagina's mine now."

He said the same things over and over, kissing me on my lips and all over my face when I cried out because his cock was so long that it hurt a little whenever he thrust himself all the way inside me. I didn't say anything back, just kissed him and held on.

It was impossible to tell how long he was inside me, talking softly in my ear and thrusting, moving me back and forth on those soft sheets until I felt like I was swinging in a hammock of clouds whenever I closed my eyes. However long it was, when he finally finished it was in a burst of total silence, and afterwards he laid on top of me for a couple of minutes before peeling himself slowly off the bed and heading into the bathroom to clean up. I stayed where I was, panting, and glanced over at the clock near the bed. It had only been a little over half an hour since I'd arrived at his room.

Still in a blissed-out daze, I gathered my clothes once Jake returned, and brought them into the bathroom so I could clean up a little before slipping back into them.

"I can't believe this," I whispered at my reflection in the mirror.

Still shaking my head, I grabbed my jeans and stepped into them. *I can't believe he just paid me three hundred dollars for half an hour of the best sex I've had with* anybody *in years.*

My thoughts earlier in the week about quitting this job eventually and looking for a real relationship seemed a little rash in that moment. Jake and other clients felt so easy—no awkward first dates, no confusion about what either of us wanted, and no real uncertainty about outcomes. Where would I even start looking for a sexually dominant man to date anyway? I didn't know that I would somehow feel more comfortable at kinky parties now than I ever had. And, God, I was *so* used to having everything my own way now. Relationships required a lot more work and a lot more compromise than sessions, that much I knew.

Jake was still naked, sitting in the same spot where I'd left him when I came out of the bathroom. He watched me without saying a word while I got ready to go. We embraced one last time behind his hotel room door. It was one A.M.

Heading home, I thought about how much I loved being on the freeways at this time of night. As I sped along the easy curves that led through downtown L.A. and toward my apartment in Hollywood, I felt like I got to enjoy a secret side of the city. The interchanges and overpasses had a smooth grace, a beauty, that during the day remained obscured by the relentless traffic. I remembered feeling this exact same kind of high after my very first shift at the Dominion. I hadn't wanted to go home afterward; I'd called a friend and insisted she let me buy us both some expensive Cuban food with the cash I'd just earned.

"Get whatever you want," I'd urged, as she'd eyed the exotic drink list before dinner.

I wouldn't have drunk any of the sweet concoctions even back when I'd been a drinker, but I did order a celebratory half-Coke, half-Dr. Pepper, large, no ice. I never drank caffeine after twelve noon anymore, so for me the soda was approximately the same as a couple of snorts of cocaine. Give or take a lesbian tryst and a couple hundred dollars.

Tonight, though, I couldn't imagine anything more satisfying than wrapping up in my terry cloth bathrobe and wrestling the cats for couch space in front of my new TV. Settling in a short while later, I looked at the blank quiet screen for a few seconds before turning it on. I wanted to relive, just a little more, the hot time I'd had with Jake, but I was worried that too much reveling could result in painful disappointment if he didn't call for a while, or ever again, for that matter.

*And, so what? It'll make you cry? Isn't this the same person who cries for most of the day before each trip to New York because she's worried that it'll hurt her cats' feelings when she leaves?* It was true; it didn't take much to set me off. Why let the possibility of one more weeping spell cramp my style tonight? If a certain amount of bum-outs were inevitable anyway—and I was pretty sure at this point in my life that they were—all the more reason to revel in the fun parts, it seemed to me now.

*Okay, you talked me into it.* I set the remote control down beside me, leaned my head back, and closed my eyes.

*Hold still.*

I heard Jake's firm, gentle voice in my head, and let it lead me where I wanted me to go.